Dear Sakinah,

Enjoy the read!

Adam Mangai

16.4.12

"Running a small business means most of my learning comes from experience rather than formal courses and this book made me realise how much of my learning in the last 17 years has been driven by my kids. I just wish Adam had written this book seventeen years ago so I could have fully benefitted from the arrival of my first child!"

- Mike Armstrong, Managing Director, The Cog Research Consultancy

"We are traditionally encouraged to leave our work at the office but very rarely to bring our family lives to work. Through anecdotes, advice (and situations that every parent will recognise with a wry smile), Adam shows how some domestic behaviours can have a positive and powerful impact on the way we work and the way we work with others".

- James Gordon-MacIntosh, parent to Imogen and Managing Partner and co-founder at Hope & Glory PR

"As a working Dad I never realised that there were so many lessons to be learnt from parenting that can be used in the workplace and vice-versa... Adam's perfectly formed book illustrates the parallels and is educational, entertaining and, best of all, engaging!"

- Robert Callway, Children's TV Director

"Far from being 'nonsense' (as the author's young daughter suggests) Adam Margolin should be relieved to learn that his approach to *Making Business Child's Play* is filled with eye-catching insights and practical strategies for managers and parents alike".

- Dr. Jonathan Reynolds, Academic Director, Oxford Institute of Retail Management

"As a new father myself, Making Business Child's Play had me nodding in agreement page after page. There are certainly some good parallels with my own experiences of both parenting and business".

- Toby Britton, Managing Director, The Flavour Media

"A quick, easy and thought provoking read. An interesting concept and undeniably we can all learn from the behaviour of children".
- *Claire Furlong, Head of Marketing and Communications, UKA*

"In this book, Adam Margolin shows us how we need to re-master the skills and techniques that we observe in our children and that we all once possessed. By identifying the parallels between what goes on at home and at work, we see how we can transfer behaviours to create a more successful, harmonious and effective workplace".
- *Laura Haynes, Chairman, Appetite*

"A useful skip through some often overlooked aspects of people management - made more memorable since we've all been experts once… but it may have been a few years ago!"
- *Mick Style, Managing Director, MEC Manchester*

"In my time at Honeypot I have been humbled and inspired by the stories of the children we help. It is great that Adam has shared his insightful knowledge and experiences in this book and I hope that it informs and inspires readers to think more creatively (as children often do!) about their journey as adults, parents and employees".
- *Richard Cooper, Corporate Partnerships Manager, Honeypot.*

"Adam has done an excellent job of identifying a common set of weaknesses in everyday business management, and giving an easy to understand context as to why there should really be no excuses".
- *Roger Siddle, Group Chief Executive, Findel*

"I can very much relate to Adam's comparisons with children and their behaviour. Making Business Child's Play is so thought-provoking, logical and full of analogies. Whether or not you have children, this book can really help you to free yourself and move forward in your career".
- *Jennifer Sawdon, Singer, Songwriter & Pianist*

"I found this book to be an enriching read from two perspectives - as a busy Managing Director, but also as an under-pressure dad. Like most great ideas, this book is based on a simple but compelling premise; that if we thought for a moment to apply aspects and principles of our home behaviours to our work behaviours, we would transform our performance for the better and to everyone's benefit. This book is packed with home-grown truths, revealed through the author's direct experience of being a father of two young children and a successful manager of grown-ups! But the real triumph of the book is its ability to reframe an array of practicable business tips and techniques using an elegant and honest narrative style, punctuated by insights from what so many of us already do naturally as parents and what comes as second nature to kids. Having read the book, I'm inspired to think differently about both my work life and my home life".
- *Stephen Bogan, Managing Director, Genesis Advertising*

"Adam's book is full of excellent skills that allow the expansion and freeing of one's imagination. This is a book full of surprises and insights. As the UK Athletics National High Jump coach currently preparing athletes for 2012, I was very interested in the chapters that gave insight into *Improving our attention* and *Dealing with fear and change*. It's a must read whether you work for a multi-national or are dreaming of starting your own business".
- *Fuzz Ahmed, National Event Coach High Jump, UKA*

"Success without the sweat… whilst not a parent, as an athlete I can relate to so much of this book. It was so punchy, even I had time to read it despite my busy training schedule".
- *Jenny Meadows, World and European 800m Medallist*

"This draws together many parallels of parenting and workplace behaviours. It made me smile as I read the examples – yes!! I'd been there too! Read and relate".
- *Steve Parkin, Managing Director, SP Group*

"Children are often an inspiration and continually help us learn by giving us startling insights. Adam has undertaken a structured analysis of his experiences and how they could be translated into more effective strategies at work, which are simple but effective. Whilst much of the read is common sense, which makes it easy to relate to, the real challenge is living it every day and not just talking about it".
- *Alison Hutchinson, CEO, The Pennies Foundation*

"In business, you are constantly making decisions and managing interactions. I am always trying to work out whether the framework within which I behave at work is learned or intuitive. Adam's book made me consider a whole new aspect of my working life: what have I forgotten that I once knew? What have I jettisoned as I have learned to fit in with working norms, and did this hold some of the answers to the perennial challenges I face? Adam not only gives entertaining examples and forensic insights – he offers a chance to re-boot and to get back in touch with the fundamental relationships that underpin our behaviour".
- *James Lowman, Chief Executive, Association of Convenience Stores*

"Having read Adam's book it's now very clear that Stanley (age 10) and Daisy (age 7) have been 'managing upward' for some years. The notion that the negotiating skills I have unwittingly honed on them might be redeployed to equal effect in the workplace is intriguing, though, not least because I have referred to my work colleagues as 'like a bunch of kids' more than once. It also goes much of the way to explaining the popularity of 'free chocolate Fridays' with my colleagues. Curly Wurly anyone? But only in exchange for best behaviour, obviously".
- *Darren Styles, Managing Director, Stream Publishing*

Making Business Child's Play

You already do it as a parent.
You used to do it as a child.
You see your children doing it.
So don't keep it confined to your home.
Harness it and use it everywhere.

Adam Margolin

ISBN 978-0-9571764-0-9

A catalogue record for this book is available from the British Library

Design and typesetting by Claire Margolin

Unless otherwise stated all images are courtesy of Adam Margolin. Any inadvertent omissions can be rectified in future editions.

www.makingbusinesschildsplay.com

For my princess and my heir...

Contents

Acknowledgements

I was giving my then three-year-old daughter Jolie dinner in the kitchen on a Saturday afternoon when I started to write this book. I had to stop mid-way through my very first sentence to take Jolie to the toilet! It occurred to me that if I could write and publish this book then anyone could achieve their goals with the right amount of resolve, commitment and support.

This book, like most books today, did not result solely from the efforts of one person. In writing this book, I am especially grateful to my family for their help, encouragement and understanding.

I have to thank my wonderful wife Elisa, first for giving me both my children, and secondly for supporting me throughout this process including allowing me time on Sunday mornings to disappear for a couple of hours to write.

I owe a great deal of thanks to my sister Claire for designing and typesetting the book, my cousin Jason for building the website that accompanies it and Craig, Lisa and Leigh for their editing prowess.

I must also give special thanks to the many family, friends and colleagues who took the time to read various drafts of my book and provide incisive, candid and constructive feedback and some fantastic supportive quotes.

I am very fortunate to have two wonderful children, Jolie and Fraser, who have taught me so much and without whom this book couldn't have been conceived and simply would not have been written.

Making Business
Child's Play

Introduction

Muhammad Ali said "children make you want to start life over". I personally wouldn't go quite that far but having children has certainly had a huge impact on my life and really made me think differently. When I started writing this book, I had been married for five years, was the proud father of a beautiful little three-year-old girl Jolie, and had an eight-months-pregnant wife. Fatherhood is a challenging, eye-opening and enlightening experience but what I never expected was to wonder why I don't approach things like Jolie or her friends. When and why did I (and other adults) lose the ability to 'behave like a child'?

A book focused on behaviours exhibited by children and parents may seem like a very strange concept for a business publication. However, the motivation and inspiration for writing this title came from personal frustration and a growing sense of how things could be different if I learnt how to stop compartmentalising my life and applying what I knew in my home life to my working identity.

Making Business Child's Play is for people looking for practical, action oriented ideas about business behaviours in an accessible entertaining style. It is written to be read in less than two hours, ideal for your next train journey or flight. It has been inspired in style and length by a number of what I believe to be hugely powerful business books including *Who moved my cheese?; The One Minute Manager; Jonathan Livingston Seagull; Feel the fear and do it anyway* and more.

It is not written as a textbook but provides lots of insights, hints and tips across a wide variety of topics through a very personal series of stories and analogies about my children and me. The book is for all types of people across all types of industries but is perfect for aspiring managers with young children working in an office environment. So, if you are interested in a book which takes a fresh innovative look at common subjects then read on. Once you have finished reading, you will have discovered an array of practical tips and techniques giving you a changed and enriched perspective as a manager and or a parent.

There are so many things that a child naturally does better than an adult and there are some behaviours that adults try desperately to recapture. The example that jumps immediately to mind is posture. Just have a look at a group of young children (up to 5 years old) and you'll notice that they move with ease and agility. Then have a look at some older kids and you will start to see some hunched shoulders. Finally, if you look at adults, you can see that these problems have fully developed. The Alexander Technique teaches people to re-establish the natural relationship between the head, the neck and the back, a relationship which can usually be seen to be working powerfully, beautifully and effortlessly in small children. Whilst the Alexander Technique has become internationally-renowned and taught all over the world, so many other behaviours which come naturally to us as children are lost as we become older and there are no techniques to help us find most of these skills again.

The flip side of the same coin is intriguing and involves looking at how we behave as parents (or teachers, carers, aunts, uncles etc.) Fatherhood has forced me to behave in a way that is designed to help my children develop and grow, and I wonder why I don't exhibit these behaviours more in the work place. If I did, how much better would things be for me and my team?

I told Jolie I was writing a book in which she was featured. I asked if she was excited and she responded "No. It's not useful. It's nonsense." I truly hope this is not the case!

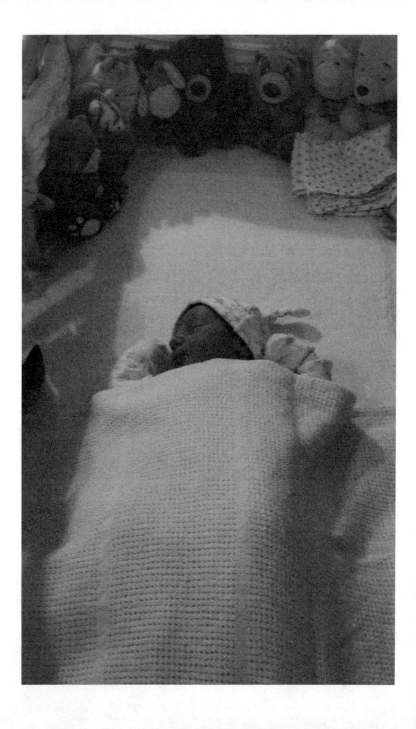

Chapter 1
Preparing for a new arrival

Before my daughter Jolie was born, my wife Elisa and I spent a long time preparing for her arrival. We had to find room in our home, which meant throwing out lots of 'essential' items and clothes to create some space for a new child.

It's amazing how we had expanded to fill the space available and yet when we needed to reorganise, it wasn't actually that hard. My parents are a great example of this in reverse. Since my sister and I have moved out, they have spread to every cupboard and room in the house, even though when we lived there they managed to confine their belongings to just their own room.

As you might be aware, children need a LOT of stuff. We had to buy a cot, sheets, bedding, sleeping bags, a rocking chair, a changer, a room thermometer, bathseats, a high chair, a buggy, clothes, muslins, dummies, bottles and the list goes on and on. We researched, discussed and agreed on every purchase and made all the necessary preparations. When Jolie was brought home from the hospital, we were ready for her. Now of course it wasn't all smooth sailing. For example, we bought a cot which I decided to build a few days before Elisa's due date. As it transpired (and yes, I should have counted the pieces first!) it was missing a side. This then had to be returned and we only just managed to get it back and build it before Jolie came home from the hospital. Nevertheless, we had prepared for her, and when she finally arrived she slotted into our home fairly naturally. Our son, Fraser's arrival was even easier as we knew what to expect, had been through it before and had a lot of what he needed already in the house.

Can you imagine bringing a child home from the hospital and only *then* considering where they might sleep? Or what they might eat, sit on or wear? Or which room they will go in? Of course not. All of this planning is carried out beforehand to make the transition for both the parents and the child as easy and as positive an experience as possible.

From my experience, this is almost always the exact opposite of what happens at work for new starters. You hire someone new to the company, and the day before they arrive, they call or email to ask what time they should come in on their first day. You panic as you realise you are in no way ready for their arrival and tell them 10am to give you some time to prepare. You rush round to IT to explain that you have a new starter who will need a computer, a desk, a chair, an email address and so on. IT are as helpful as ever and tell you that there is a minimum one-week lead time (if not three weeks!) needed for all such requests but they will do the best they can to accommodate you. You then realise that you haven't prepared an induction programme or even a set of documents to read and so you desperately try to get meetings in people's diaries and any information printed out and shoved into a ring binder. The next day your poor new member of staff arrives to be greeted with a fairly brief office tour and a series of introductions to people they won't remember. You don't show them how to log into their computer (if they have one) or how to dial an outside line on their phone. You don't tell them what they are expected to do and you are probably in meetings "you can't get out of" for most of the day which means you sit them in a seat which is probably not actually at their new desk and hand them a folder of semi-relevant information to read.

What a terrible first impression to make, and that new starter is probably already questioning why they accepted the position. A few days later, if they are lucky, they have finally met a few relevant people, been set up properly with all the necessary equipment and can actually start their new job. What a waste of time, effort and money and what a shame that you haven't harnessed the time when that new member of staff is most keen to learn and impress.

The solution is really simple. You should look at this new employee as an opportunity to show off your company. As managers (and as an organisation) you will never get a second chance to make a first impression. As such you have to spend time and effort preparing for a new employee's arrival to help ensure they are successful in their role.

In the USA, the process of a new starter being set up properly within a company is called employee "onboarding". It is designed to ensure that the new starter feels wanted, relaxed, equipped and supported. These positive feelings will undoubtedly increase the chances of the new starter making an impact in the short, medium and long term. And what's more, the happier and more satisfied the employee is, the more successful they are likely to be and the longer they should remain with the company.

To position a new starter for success is actually very easy and all you really need to think about is what you would like a new job to be like. Before they start you need to have prepared for their arrival. You should plan a thorough induction process with meetings set up with key members of the team. You should provide your colleagues with a full briefing on what you expect your new starter to get out of the meeting and should give your colleagues a copy of the new starter's CV and job specification. Each meeting should follow a similar format and include a summary of their own position, where there are overlaps between their role and the new starter's role and any expectations for working together going forward. You should also spend some time preparing to explain the company culture, goals and ways of working so they can settle in as easily as possible.

Next, and in some ways, most importantly, you have to set up a comfortable place for them to live. You may think this is a funny choice of words, but we spend a huge amount of time at work and we have to want to be there and feel comfortable where we sit. This is no different to bringing a new child home from the hospital having ensured they will be comfortable in their new home. For your new starter, you have to ensure that when they arrive their workstation is completely set up. This will involve ensuring their computer/laptop is waiting for them with an email address and log in details. They will need a phone with voicemail activated as well as pens, paper and any other stationery or equipment required to help them hit the ground running, including a staff telephone directory, organisational charts and employee handbooks. In an ideal world, you should also provide them with business cards. I don't think I have ever met anyone who had any business cards within the first month of starting a new job. This is actually crazy when all we need to know is their name, title and contact details, and we know all this before they set foot in the building! Finally, a few freebies never go amiss! What I mean by this is giving the new starter some company branded t-shirts, mugs, key rings, a hat, a backpack, USB sticks and so on. These items are probably floating around anyway but they will really make the new employee feel wanted and welcome. It is also essential that all administrative forms (pensions, direct debits, life insurance, health insurance, next of kin etc.) are all ready to be completed in the first few days. This will get all the dull administrative work out of the way early.

When a baby is born, normally the mother and father are there to meet and greet their new arrival along with a whole set of friendly and helpful doctors and nurses. In a similar way, on your new starter's first day, make sure you are there to greet them personally and ensure you have cleared a good amount of time in your schedule. If this is not possible, then ensure you have fully briefed one of your team to do this in your place. Once you have greeted your new starter, show them where they are going to live (i.e. their workstation and area) and then take them on an office tour, making sure you introduce them to as many people as possible as well as showing them where the toilets, photocopiers, mail room and coffee machine are. Do not expect them to remember anyone or anything and be willing to show them again later, as starting a new job can be nerve racking, even for experienced professionals, and they have to try and absorb a huge amount of information in a very short period of time.

Try and balance the first day between meetings, orientation and informal get-togethers. I always think it is nice to try and take the new starter for lunch with a group of their new colleagues (your treat!) Finally, set up a meeting with the new starter and take them through their objectives, responsibilities and ideally what you want them to achieve in their first 100 days.

Once the first day is over, the rest of the week should focus on interactions and information exchange between the new starter and key people across the organisation as well as with external agencies and other relevant stakeholders. In this week, you should be discussing management style and ways of working and ensuring if they have any direct reports, that they are doing the same. This week should also cover the induction programme you arranged before their arrival.

The induction programme and training are absolutely vital. They will ensure that new starters settle in quickly, are happy, productive and ultimately retained. It must involve more than just skills training and has to cover the basics that you would take for granted. For example, if you finish early on a Friday in the summer or have dress-down Fridays, tell them! The induction will reinforce their decision to come and work for you. I would suggest that the induction programme is not entirely spoon-fed but does include some 'GAAFOFY' (go away and find out for yourself) methods as this will encourage the new starter to show initiative and be proactive.

This commitment, although potentially time consuming, must not end after the first week. It is important that you take as many opportunities as possible to integrate the new starter into the company during the first three months (and beyond), whether via social events, committees or work groups. There is no doubt that the investment of time and effort during this initial period will pay back time and time again as the career of your new starter flourishes.

It is also vital that at the end of the first 100 days there is formal two-way feedback between the new starter and their direct line manager. This meeting could involve a member of the HR department and should be used to raise issues and concerns as well as positive feedback. The outcome should ensure that the new starter is ready for success in their role. Feedback is important throughout the process, whether on behaviours, company culture, strategy or ways of working and/or suggestions that could improve or change the ways things are done. New starters always bring with them a range of valuable experiences and new ideas and these should be harnessed.

One thing that has become clear from having two children is the desire for friends and family to visit on a constant basis (often irritatingly so!) When Jolie and Fraser were born, people came to the hospital and to our house to bring presents and more importantly to meet the newest arrival. They want to hold the baby, give him/her kisses and cuddles and support us as parents. A friend of mine (admittedly a talented home economist) actually made a whole freezer full of meals for her best friend when she had a baby so she wouldn't have to worry about cooking when the baby came home. It is amazing how kind, supportive and generous people can be.

In comparison, a new starter at work is not normally met with anywhere near the same level of kindness. More often than not, after an amicable greeting, the new starter is left to fend for his or herself in the corner. This reminds me a lot of when new kids start at school and the other children often take a long time to let them into their friendship groups. Of course as managers we can't force our team to like a new starter but we should certainly be encouraging them to exhibit friendly, welcoming behaviour if we hope to progress with a well oiled team. If at work, people made a real effort to get to know the new starter, to offer their time and expertise to help and support them and to make them feel welcome and ensure they land on their feet, these new starters would be firing on all cylinders much more quickly.

The manager should also not be forgotten and in a similar way, colleagues should ask how they are doing and offer to help and support. Are there projects that are struggling because of the time required to train the newest team member? Is it their first ever direct report and do they know what they are doing? Across the business there will be many people who can help but often are either not willing or probably just haven't thought about it.

I really struggled with my first direct report, Jess. It was hard to find time for her and I found the experience and process of managing someone stressful and difficult. I turned to a friend and colleague, Jo, who was at a similar level in a different department but had much more experience when it came to managing a team. Effectively, and unofficially, she became my coach and mentor. She helped me through difficult situations, she advised me on techniques she had put in place to get the most out of her team and she helped me when it came to discipline and control. I am forever grateful for her help. Now I have managed a variety of people with differing backgrounds, races, religions, beliefs, desires, motivations and so on. No two people are the same and as a manager I have to try and understand my team as well as I can. The one thing I try and do nowadays is to coach the people who work for me and with me, who have people to manage. I devote a lot of time to my team and my colleagues and try to support them so that they can get the most out of work, themselves and their team.

Chapter 2
Finding the time

With Jolie we realised very quickly that the opportunity to do what we wanted to do and behave in the way we wanted to behave was greatly diminished. There was far less time for ourselves and suddenly there was a little girl who had to come first. This was a bit of a shock to the system. We had to feed her six times a day (to start with), including in the middle of the night. We had to bath her, dress her, play with her, get her to stop crying, get her to sleep, take her out for fresh air and so on. Everything took longer, especially leaving the house! However, fairly quickly a new routine was forged and it was like she had always been part of our lives. When Fraser arrived, the routine had to be altered again and the only major difference was that any free time (minimal as it was) effectively disappeared.

Once we have children, we have no choice but to change our daily routines. Everything we had to do before, from paperwork to tidying the house still has to happen but we have to find the time to do so whilst also finding the time to look after our children. This places a huge number of demands on our time and almost every day my wife says "There are just not enough hours in the day to do everything I need to do!" However, we adapt and I now realise how much we can achieve within the same amount of time.

Some of the ways in which we adapt are so obvious, instinctive and easy. What is strange is the fact that in a variety of other situations, including at work, we struggle to manage our time as effectively. The American inventor Thomas Edison said "Time is really the only capital any human being has and the one thing he can't afford to waste". Time management is a challenge for us all and there are a number of things we do with our children that can help with this dilemma throughout our lives.

Prioritisation is a really obvious place to start. As a parent, the minute Jolie was born, she became priority number one. I know when looking after my kids what has to be done and what tasks are more important, of the highest value and cannot move. We are better at juggling time for our kids because they can't wait or be put off until tomorrow and require an urgency which we don't carry across to the way we work. However, at work prioritisation is even more important. Sometimes it can be really hard to prioritise, especially when everything seems urgent. However, with our children we manage to prioritise and we understand if something is urgent or important, and we avoid focusing purely on the urgent.

In order to prioritise, you first have to know what needs to be done. I, like most people, have a to-do list, which is designed to help me remember to carry out all my necessary tasks. The problem I have found is that, more often than not, my to-do list is a random collection of tasks that have to be done at some stage. The list is in no particular order and as a result I have a tendency to focus on the tasks I know will be easier, quicker or those that I enjoy doing more. Prioritisation involves ordering the to-do list by understanding which tasks are important and will add the most value. By focusing efficiently on these tasks, you won't get caught rushing round last minute trying to get things done. A well managed to-do list will help you tackle the most important jobs first, reduce time wasted on more trivial tasks and reduce the stress generated by a long list of fairly unimportant jobs. A simple example in our house when Fraser was young involved sterilising his bottles. I knew that this task was highly important and valuable but it was dull and tedious. It involved cleaning all the bottles, sterilising them, filling the kettle, boiling it, waiting until the bottles were cool enough to handle and the water was cool enough to pour and then filling each bottle to the appropriate level before putting the various parts together (i.e. lid, teat and the two other bits I don't know what to call!) It also involved filling the milk powder containers with the right amount of powder for the bottles. This might all sound a bit futile. However, when I forgot to prioritise this task and Fraser went hysterical because he needed a feed and we didn't have any bottles, it didn't seem so futile! Doing this task early removed all the stress that might arise later and allowed me to move on to other tasks. So if you are creating a to-do list at work, I would suggest you write your list, then go back through it and mark the importance of the task from 1 (important) to 5 (unimportant) and then re-order the list into one of importance and start ticking them off one at a time from the top. This will ensure that the most important and beneficial tasks are completed first and none of your colleagues will be go hysterical.

One thing that all parents try to achieve is to get their children, especially babies, onto a schedule. When both Jolie and Fraser were small, we tried hard to get them onto a 7am, 11am, 3pm, 7pm, 11pm, 3am feeding schedule. After a few months, the 3am disappears and then the 11pm disappears and weaning begins so the schedule adapts to incorporate food at 11.30am and 5.30pm and so on. To me, managing a family with children is all about routine and schedules as they give structure to the day and an understanding of what tasks have to be done and when. Similarly at work, if you know what your goals and priorities are, you can create a schedule that keeps you (and everyone else) on track, thus reducing stress in the long term and making sure your work "family" is on track to grow and progress. If you have never created a schedule, it can seem like a daunting task but it is actually much easier than you probably think. All you really need to know is the time you have available and the tasks you need to do. Then start by putting in the essential jobs that you have to do, add important or urgent tasks and any admin that is vital to your role. Then add in the other jobs that you need or want to do.

It is important to realise, however, that schedules have to be flexible and fluid. We have friends who wouldn't go out in the afternoon because their children were taking a nap and they had to sleep in their cot. In contrast, we made sure that Jolie's sleep patterns were flexible and as a result we have a child who will sleep anywhere when she is tired. Whilst in this example the reward of being flexible with Jolie is that she will sleep anywhere, the reward for you and your team being flexible is that you will all excel at time management.

It can be extremely hard to leave the house on schedule with two young children. More often than not something unexpected happens, whether that is one of them needing the toilet, being sick or having forgotten something. At work there are often meetings and projects that will impact on your time so whilst you can focus on priority tasks, you have to leave contingency time in any schedule for unexpected events and interruptions that would otherwise create chaos.

Another thing that I have had to try and master as a parent is managing distractions and interruptions, especially when trying to work from home. Distractions come in the form of my bed, the sofa, computer games, Sky+ or wanting to play with my children when there are chores to do, whilst interruptions involve giving Jolie attention because she needs a drink, the toilet, her dinner, a bath or more often than not because she has hurt herself in some way! At work distractions and interruptions will include emails, phone calls or information requests and they prevent us getting into the 'zone' which is where we are fully engaged in a task and its completion is pretty easy. Whilst some of these interruptions need to be dealt with immediately, others need to be managed. It is vital to minimise distractions in order to take control of your day (or part of your day) and get things done. At home, this may require turning off the TV, your phone or instant messenger and telling your family that you need to focus on something and they need to leave you in peace. It could involve listening to music or it may involve setting others a task (e.g. asking Jolie to make me a card or something out of bricks or Play Doh) or distracting them with something they enjoy (e.g. letting Jolie play in the garden or sitting her in front of CBeebies). Whilst we must accept that distractions or interruptions are a natural and necessary part of life, we have to find a way of managing them and being able to get back into the flow quickly afterwards in order to drive our own efficiency.

Procrastination is the downfall of many, including my wife. (Let's hope she isn't reading this!) It involves putting off until later jobs that could (and maybe should) be completed now. It can also include putting off more important and difficult tasks in favour of smaller, easier tasks and it is something we all do. The best way to beat it is to recognise when you are about to procrastinate and avoid doing so by pushing yourself harder to break the habit, whilst reminding yourself of the implications if you do procrastinate. Then use positive reinforcement on yourself to force this 'good behaviour' by rewarding yourself for getting jobs done. These rewards do not have to be costly or complicated. When Jolie was little, she would try and put off tidying her bedroom and getting in the bath. However, as this task often fell close to bedtime, we were able to reward her with stories or threaten less stories if she didn't comply. After a while, she stopped procrastinating and tidied up her room and got into the bath straight away.

One of the most important skills at work or at home is organisation. Something that becomes really difficult with children is being on time, and at work punctuality is hugely important and something that I have struggled with. In an attempt to use every available moment to maximise my efficiency, I am often late. I should be sitting in the boardroom waiting for my Managing Director to arrive five minutes before the meeting is due to begin (already with my cup of tea), however more often than not I skate in just as it's beginning.

Organisation is both mental and physical and whilst it involves to-do lists and prioritisation, it also involves considering how you arrange the physical space around you to enhance your performance and efficiency. I have lost count of the number of times Jolie has asked for something just as we are leaving the house (in the summer, always her sunglasses) and being organised is critical in knowing where everything is. At work, a messy desk, drawers, email inbox or business card holder can affect your productivity as you will waste valuable time searching for something instead of being able to tick something off your to-do list. Becoming organised is a difficult task but staying organised may actually be even tougher so it is something we all have to work on every day. In a strange way, staying organised becomes part of a good routine. For example, I tidy Jolie and Fraser's playroom every night so that the next morning she can make it messy again. Why? Because the time I don't, she will desperately want or need something and I won't know where it is! Falling out of this routine, even for one night, puts me on a downward spiral. Staying organised will reduce stress levels and keep us healthy and so we have to do it, even when we really don't want to!

At work, there are a few things I would suggest that can help you be more organised. First, only save what you must. When I used to receive lots of physical post, I was pretty good at glancing through it to determine if it should be kept, filed or binned. With my emails, I am much more relaxed and keep far more than I should. This clutters my email account and actually slows down my computer. Secondly, save attachments from your emails onto your computer. When doing so, follow one way of naming the files or folders and store related documents together, both in your emails and in project folders. When a project has been completed, try and sort through everything and only keep the final versions of any files (if any). Try to avoid putting too much in folders as these become difficult to manage and harder to find anything within. It is important to make sub folders to whatever level is necessary to make managing the files easy, understandable and quick. Finally, make sure that you back up your files and folders, just in case something goes horribly wrong. This is often automatic in big companies. In smaller businesses it can be a little time consuming but is very important.

One thing that changed automatically when I became a parent was my attitude. I want to see my children grow, develop, learn, be healthy and happy and so I have become much more motivated to carry out the mundane tasks involved in making this happen. At work, it is sometimes much more difficult to motivate yourself but self-motivation is extremely important in maximising productivity and time management. Learn what motivates you to do your best work and then try to create an environment that supports this.

If you spend too much time doing work that other people could do, and you have no time to progress your own objectives, then you need to re-consider the roles and responsibilities within your team. When Jolie reached an age where she could understand and complete tasks on her own, we started to delegate to her. This allowed us, as a family, to be even more productive as we divided and conquered the tasks at hand. For example, when we went to the park, whereas originally I would have had to get everything ready myself, Jolie put her shoes and socks on and even helped get things for Fraser from his room. Elisa and I are always delegating tasks to each other to maximise our time and efficiency. For example, she will say "You change Fraser's nappy and I will get his bag ready". Although this example may seem simplistic, it actually highlights a key element within effective delegation which is the difference between someone doing your work for you and ensuring the right person performs the task. In this instance, because

Elisa gets Fraser's bag ready every day, she is much better at it than I am and therefore this is the right task for her to complete. We are equally good at changing his nappy and therefore this becomes my task.

At work, this is even more important. To be truly productive, you must rely on the team around you to help. If managed correctly, you should be able to achieve much more as a team than you could as an individual. It is also important to remember that delegation involves supporting and giving someone all the help and resources they require to complete the task. It does not involve micromanaging the process or the person or making sure things are done your way. I have really struggled in this area as I like things to be done a certain way and can be a bit of a control freak. However, I am learning that to delegate successfully, I have to let go and trust other people to do the job well. I am doing this more and more with my team and the result is a motivated team of people who support each other and have a much greater level of productivity.

Something that I personally have had to become much better at is multi-tasking. When researching this book I found several studies which found that multi-tasking can result in us wasting between 20-40% of our time and concluded that it isn't a more efficient use of time and doesn't make us more productive. I understand why this might be the case as, when trying to multi-task we often start a lot of tasks which makes each one take longer than it should have done. Having said that, I do believe that multi-tasking is vital, especially for anyone trying to balance work and home life. I am a strong believer in having a good work-life balance and try to leave work at a reasonable time every day so I can be home for my children's dinner, bath and bed time. More often than not however, I haven't finished working for the day when I get home and sometimes it is just nice to be able to sit at my kitchen table whilst Jolie and Fraser eat their dinner and check my emails or finish off some work. This is multi-tasking as I am managing to feed my children, spend time with them and check my emails all at the same time.

Chapter 3
Learning new things

Children have a passion to learn. At three if Jolie said something incorrectly or mispronounced a word and I corrected her, she immediately repeated back the correct pronunciation until she knew it. Her attitude was totally different to most adults. If I correct a colleague in a similar way, they get defensive and take this as a personal slight. But what should we teach our children? How should we teach them? How do we give them new experiences? We are always telling Jolie to try new things and foods and when she says "no" we ask her how she knows if she doesn't like it if she hasn't tried it. At work, I think we underestimate how passionate most people are about learning and developing new skills, especially if they will further their careers as a result.

When we had both Jolie and Fraser, we were given a great deal of information (by friends, family, health visitors, the hospital and books) which explained to us how our children should be developing month by month, stage by stage. As our children have developed, we refer to this information and continually compare them with others to see if their behaviours are 'normal' and whether they are developing faster or slower than others.

I have brought this insight into my working life and now 360 degree evaluations and appraisals form the basis of how I manage people. If you are not aware of what I mean by this, it is basically feedback from a number of sources (employees, peers, managers and external colleagues) who work with the person you are asking for feedback about. It also includes self assessment and it is really interesting to assess someone's self awareness by comparing their answers to those that others write about them. From my experience, people are pretty self aware and expect the feedback they receive with one or two notable exceptions which need to be discussed. The benefit of using this method of gathering feedback is that it ensures a rounded view from a variety of people and not just you as a manger who only actually sees them for a small percentage of the time. As an example, the following are the questions I normally ask when conducting a 360 degree appraisal:

1. Does X complete tasks quickly and efficiently?
2. Does X show good initiative and the ability to handle projects with minimum direction?
3. Does X produce work to a high standard every time?
4. Is X an effective team player?
5. Do you feel X has passion for the role and for the brand/business?
6. Do you think X fits in well with the company culture?
7. How well does X communicate with you or with others?
8. What are X's strengths?
9. What are X's development areas?
10. What do you think is the most important thing that X could focus on to drive their career forward in the next 6 months?

Once I have received all the responses, I summarise an answer to each question as well as providing some key verbatim statements and an overall summary at the end. I will then spend one to two hours discussing the feedback, normally off-site, with the aim of agreeing key development areas and training plans.

Parents' evenings provide us with an opportunity to hear feedback from teachers and to understand how our children are getting on compared to their peers. Even at nursery school, Jolie's teachers have a detailed curriculum, which shows what skills a child should be developing and how he or she should be behaving throughout his or her time at school. In a similar way, I strongly believe that every employee should have a clear set of objectives for the short, medium and long term. I originally worried that this might be stating the obvious as most companies would agree and would be doing this. However, from my experience and research this is unfortunately not the case.

I also think it is important to have a set of competencies which exist across an organisation. Competency frameworks are designed to explain the 'how' and not the 'what' people should be doing. They should be objective measures designed to assess potential as well as supporting the development of individuals through an understanding of what behaviours or skills are expected within each role and how they can be attained. Applied consistently across an organisation will ensure employees feel they are being treated fairly and 'apples are being compared to apples'. They will make clear which of your team are performing at the right level, who your 'stars' are and who needs development. This will then make it easier to decide how and when to help someone learn something new.

What I think we all forget as managers is that the people working for us are striving to achieve and if we spend time helping them at the beginning, it will pay dividends and save us time and effort in the long run. When Jolie was three, I took her to the park and decided it was time to tackle the rope ladder. She was afraid at first and wanted to stick to the swings and the slide. In other words, she wanted to stay within her comfort zone. However, I took her to the rope ladder and showed her how to climb it. I demonstrated twice and then I held her and positioned her feet as she climbed it herself. After about 10 minutes, she was happily climbing on her own. Now she needs no help or support and has actually shown her friends how to do it.

Weaning is another great example of persistence and perseverance when teaching our children new things. When Fraser was four months old, we started to wean him. This involved starting him on solid foods for the first time and required him to eat off a spoon when all he had ever known was how to drink from a bottle. For Fraser, this must have been a really strange experience as at first he had no idea what to do with the spoon and spat out the first mouthful of food, as it was new, different and a little odd, and so he rejected it. Obviously, as parents, we need our children to learn to eat, so we fed Fraser again and again, once a day, twice a day, until he learnt how to eat from a spoon.

During weaning, Elisa made a huge variety of different foods (baby rice, carrot, pear puree etc.) with different textures in order to help Fraser try new things and to help us understand what he really liked. Since birth all he had known was milk but there were some foods, flavours and textures he loved and others he naturally and instinctively didn't like. Throughout the process we effectively forced Fraser to try new things and have new experiences.

Even once Fraser and Jolie had started to eat solid food we would still break it up into bitesized chunks to enable them to swallow and digest the food more easily. Breaking up a task into smaller more manageable bits is a great way of approaching any new task whether at home or at work.

I wonder again why we don't exhibit this behaviour more in the work place. When we are asked to do things we have never done before, or when we ask a member of our team to do something new and different, they are often resistant to this new opportunity. So many of us are content to stay within our comfort zones as we believe 'it is better the devil you know'. Effectively, we spit it out. At work, this food is then normally eaten by someone else and we are never encouraged to learn to use the spoon or try something new. But we should be. As managers we need to help "wean" our teams onto new tasks in a similar way. We should break things into bite sized parts and get them to try things little and often rather than trying to get them to change everything at once, them rejecting it and then never approaching it again.

When I think about it, I realise that even since weaning Jolie our behaviour hasn't changed. We continually encourage (and at times force) Jolie to try and experience new things. We have taken her to the theatre, the cinema, the zoo, the park, the aquarium, Legoland, Disneyland Paris, the beach, soft play, restaurants, picnics and the list goes on. At first children have a natural desire to experience new things but as they get older, even by the age of three, they become more reluctant and want to stick to what they know. I believe one of our roles as parents is to keep trying to introduce new experiences. Sometimes we have to repeat some of these experiences as we know that our children will eventually learn to enjoy them. For example, I took Jolie to the cinema to see *Shrek 4*. Despite lollypops and treats, we only lasted about half the film as it was a bit dark and scary for her (and she kept kicking the seat in front!) When we got home she told my wife that she "liked the big screen, but didn't like the movie". At three, Jolie didn't like the dark and scary parts of films (or programmes) and was not patient enough to wait to see the happy ending. However, she claimed to really like the cinema. So a while later, I picked a much lighter and more positive film and tried *Toy Story 3* and we made it through the whole movie. Sometimes at work, we have to keep pushing and encouraging our team to keep persevering with tasks that we know they will learn to enjoy.

Sometimes people are very passionate about their own personal development and it is important to harness this passion. Jolie had a passion for dance and so we decided to send her to ballet classes. Obviously this came at a cost as many training courses at work will do. We can choose to send our teams on courses to help them negotiate, influence, persuade, lead, present, speak publicly or sell recommendations. Doing so will strengthen their skills and encourage them to view the company as one that cares about their future success. This is certainly a cost worth offsetting and should help keep staff turnover rates lower. If an employee feels a company is investing in them, they are more likely to stick around.

Having said that, one of the contributing factors to my willingness to keep taking Jolie to the cinema was the fact that Vue cinemas put on Kids:AM viewings at £1 per person per film. So in essence, the risk of failure (i.e. leaving before the film finishes) was acceptable because the cost was minimal. At work, I have found a variety of ways of learning and developing myself and my team for free. Whilst there are a huge number of very expensive training courses that I can send my team on, it is amazing how many free seminars are also available. Some are in exchange for meeting with suppliers, others are put on by industry bodies and some are offered because the organisers want representatives from a variety of companies and industries in order to be able to market the event to others. More often than not, they come back energised and always pick up two or three ideas which are applicable to their job or the company in general.

There are actually lots of ways of helping to develop people at work that require only time and no financial investment. One way is to give them on-the-job coaching and experience away from their standard working routine. This might involve mentoring, taking them to customers or suppliers, attaching them to other project teams, encouraging them to attend internal briefings, facilitating work shadowing programmes with people you want them to learn from (internally or externally), job-swapping or even seconding people somewhere for a few weeks or months to develop their exposure, skills and knowledge.

Often within a business there are committees that people can join to help drive a certain aspect of the organisation. When I worked at General Mills, early on in my career, I was encouraged to join the Vision and Values Committee, whose job was to drive the company's vision and values deeper into the organisation. Being part of this team helped me develop good cross-functional relationships with a variety of people (including senior management), raised my profile within the organisation and gave me experiences I would not otherwise have gained, including event management. Whilst working at SPAR, I volunteered to join both a Think Tank as part of the Association of Convenience Stores and the Corporate Development Board of the NSPCC. All these roles were fantastic experiences and as a result, I now encourage my team to join internal and or external teams.

When my daughter first looked like she was going to walk, my wife and I were very excited. We did not however, sit her on a chair, explain to her the principle of walking, walk across to the other side of the room and say "Come on, get up, walk" and then get annoyed when she fell flat on her face. This may sound obvious. I hope it does.

So what did we do? Support, encourage, help and guide. This meant that before she could walk, in fact before she had even considered walking, we would help her stand up, we would hold her hands and walk her, we would put her in walkers to allow her to walk while supported. When she first pulled herself up on her own, we got very excited and told her how happy we were with her and how clever she was. Then over the next few days as she started to pull herself up on the furniture, stand unsupported, walk a few steps and so on, we continually encouraged her and supported her every move. Finally, after a few weeks, we had a child who walked and soon after a child who walked with confidence. The challenge now is to stop her walking off, but we will come back to that later.

This was absolutely identical to how we approached potty training. We did not explain the principle of using the toilet, remove her nappy, put knickers on her and wish her luck. We explained to her what was happening and why and we actually let her run around with no knickers on and accepted that there might be some accidents. We were not annoyed about this. We did not shout at her because she didn't know any better. We tried to create a positive and supportive atmosphere within which she could learn. And with help, support and positive reinforcement she was potty trained within 5 days, with only two accidents.

I would argue that we don't treat the people we work with and more specifically the people who work for us with the same level of respect and support. We brief or train people badly, assume they know more than they do and then when they make mistakes, we get annoyed and blame them. We should actually blame ourselves as managers.

I was discussing this with a friend, Lisa, and her view was that as we are intelligent adults, we shouldn't need as much help and support. I don't subscribe to this at all. If you have never done something before, why wouldn't you need help and training?

For example, if you ask someone to write an agency brief and they have never written a brief, is it surprising that they write it badly or get a bad response from the agency? Of course not. Could we do it ourselves quicker and better? Of course. But this doesn't help anyone in the long term. If we worked through the process, the parts of the brief, let them have a go and then went through it in detail, metaphorically holding their hand and walking them through the process would we get a better result? Of course we would. The challenge is finding the time to do so. However, if this employee was your daughter learning to walk or use the toilet you would find the time and would feel proud when he or she achieved their goal.

We have to be willing to allow our staff to fall over in order to help them learn and develop. We have to accept that the first few times, they will probably fall flat on their face or have 'an accident'. However, it is only through making these mistakes and with positive encouragement to persevere that they will conquer the task. We need to build this learning into the timings for a project or start them off on less important projects where we do not mind if there are some problems as we will have the opportunity to fix them before it is too late.

Having a direct report is actually very similar to having a child in this and many other respects. If we try and continue to put ourselves first and the needs of our direct report second, it will only end in disaster. We have to adapt and ensure that they get the amount of time they need to learn, feel supported and develop. This is even more paramount at the beginning of the relationship and at the start of any new project. This can be really difficult as often having one or more team members means that much more is expected of you and your team. You have more people and thus can deliver more. This puts great strain on your own time as it will take a while for any new team member to understand the business, become efficient and add real value. In the short term, we have to pick up the slack.

The reality is that most of us don't spend the right amount of time with our team, we don't give them the support they require and they do not come first. We fail to realise that if they did, our lives would actually be easier in the long term. We see them as a necessary burden and we behave as such. We wonder if we have to meet with our team all the time to help them do their work, how can we do our own work?

What we have to do is try to put our team first. We have to set up regular one-to-ones, and we have to try and keep these in the diary and give them the amount of time they require. If we can't, then it is our responsibility as managers to either rearrange or find another way of ensuring our team is supported. I am by no means perfect and struggle with this on a daily basis. There are times when I don't manage to have a proper one-to-one with any of my team in weeks because of holidays, bank holidays or meetings, and it is not acceptable. Sometimes it is just not possible to spend four or five hours in consecutive one-to-ones. However, this does not mean that we should not catch up at all. The solution I would suggest is to focus on the top three issues with each team member. Don't make the meetings overly formal but catch up over coffee or lunch or just have a quick 15-minute chat to ensure that any burning concerns are highlighted. As a manager, you do not want these to pop up later. The harsh truth is that it is only by giving our teams and children time and support that they can learn and develop.

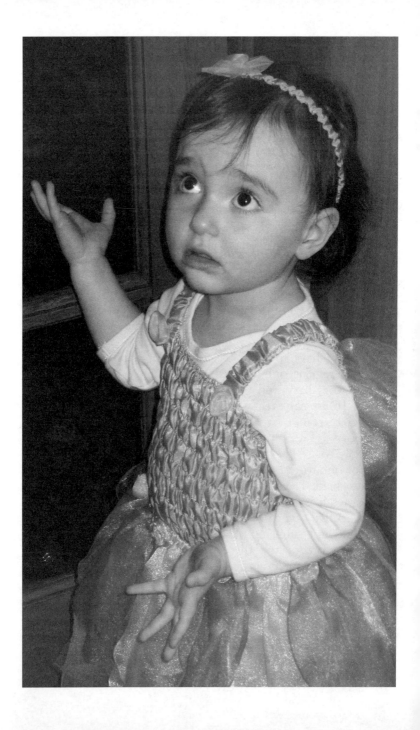

Chapter 4
Asking why?

Bright and early one morning, Jolie asked me randomly "Daddy, can we go to the beach today?" I said "No Jolie". She asked "Why?" I said "Because you have nursery school today". "Well can we go after nursery school?" Elisa got involved with "No Jolie". The response, "Why mummy?" Elisa decided to give her a rational answer "Because there are no beaches near here sweetheart". Jolie pondered this for a second "But there are beaches in France. So can we go to France?" I said "I would love to Jolie but it's not that easy to just go to France". Again, "Why?" was the response. "Because daddy has to work and we have to go on an aeroplane and we don't have any tickets". Jolie being helpful suggested "We could buy some tickets". And this went on and on... Why? Why? Why?

Being asked "Why?" by Jolie was a hugely infuriating experience. When she turned three, the floodgates seemed to open and she started to ask me "Why?" about everything. "Why is the grass green?" "Why are you going to work?" "Why are you not coming home tonight Daddy, do you not want to read me a story?" "Why do I have to be good?" And most of the time, whatever answer I gave, she was never satisfied. I realised that I got frustrated for two reasons. First, because I didn't always know the answer to her questions and secondly, because even if I could answer, she had more questions to follow.

However, sometimes you have to invite questions, especially when presenting information, in order to check everyone understands what you are trying to get across. Whilst you can try and think through what the other person might ask and try to answer the questions up front, there is always undoubtedly something that you haven't thought of. Often questions provide an opportunity to add information and opinions that you didn't include. If you are presenting, it is sensible to make clear up front whether you are willing to take questions throughout or at a specific point (normally the end). If you are a more inexperienced or nervous presenter, I would suggest always taking questions at the end. This is because if you invite questions at any point and an impromptu discussion kicks off in the middle of your presentation, it is hard to regain control.

It is important however, to try and consider what questions you might be asked. If you know there is an elephant in the room that no one wants to discuss, then it may be sensible to bring the subject up yourself. Be confident and try and tackle any issues head on. By avoiding certain topics, what we do more often than not is cause ourselves problems later on.

Questions get asked for lots of different reasons. Some are very positive reasons which will normally involve people wanting to find out more, to show support or to clarify something for themselves and others. However, occasionally, people will use the opportunity to ask a question to challenge, publicly embarrass you, to try and demonstrate weakness or to even get their own point across. If a question makes you feel like you are being attacked, it is very easy to become defensive and even aggressive. However, it is vital that you try and remove your emotions from the situation, stay calm and rational when responding. A great technique I was taught is to diffuse the situation with humour or disarm the person asking by complimenting them on their great question. Never get sucked in, just answer and move on (and maybe curse them at home later!)

But what about handling questions we can't answer? The danger is that if we can't answer one question then people might think that there are lots of holes in our arguments, even if they aren't sure where they might be. I learned quickly with Jolie that if I am unable to answer the question, she will keep asking and quickly discover that I don't know. The solution is not to lie or try to pretend I know more than I do but to be honest if I don't know the answer. I say I will try and find out or I bridge to another topic by saying "I'm sorry, I don't know. But what I can tell you is…" How to answer a question when you don't know the answer really depends on how you are feeling at the time. If you are feeling confident and believe that the audience sees you as credible then you can probably just admit you don't know. If you don't feel that this is appropriate, then you can say that you have the information elsewhere and that you and the person asking should take the topic offline. It is also important to differentiate between questions, comments, observations or just someone else's view as the latter often don't actually need an answer.

I have also learned never to rush to answer questions, even if I predicted the question and know the answer. I was actually told this originally when being given interview tips. Take your time, take a few breaths and demonstrate that you are considering the answer to the question by putting on a pondering look, nodding slowly and looking up and to the left. Then answer and when you are happy that you have answered the question, stop speaking. Try not to keep talking as eventually you will talk yourself into trouble. It is important to remember that if the person who asked the question doesn't think they have been answered sufficiently, they will follow up to try and understand further but if they have been answered, then the quicker and more succinctly you can do it, the better.

When dealing with Jolie, the more questions I answered, the more I realised that she didn't necessarily mean "Why?" in the way I originally thought she did. Although her language had developed extremely well and she spoke like an adult (worryingly at times) she was actually using the word "Why?" as a short hand for asking generally about a subject. She was showing interest and wanted to talk about it more with me, because she trusted and loved me. The answer didn't have to give a reason or start with "Because" but could actually just involve exploring the topic in greater detail.

Asking why is all about showing curiosity and is critical to almost any decision making, planning or brainstorming activity. Curiosity can jump start the creative process by making us ask questions, explore options and go beyond where we are currently to something better. Jolie and her friends are always asking why and finding creative solutions to problems, whereas at work, we are often willing to just accept the situation or only improve things marginally. A great example that springs to mind happened just after I started at SPAR. The point-of-sale approval process was explained to me and I was told how much better it had become because we were now using three physical books (full of artwork to approve) instead of one. This streamlined the process and gave each approver more time to review and sign off their artwork. I started to ask why and the answers helped us see some obvious ways to improve the process. The result was the building of a web-based digital solution which required no paper and was much faster.

I was once taught that if we ask ourselves "Why?" five times and can give a clear answer at the end, we will have absolute clarity. I have since learnt that this concept was actually made popular in the 1970s by the Toyota Production System. It is an easy, effective and hugely beneficial technique which can help all of us truly understand why we want to do something or why we are asking someone else to do something.

As a marketeer, asking why helps me understand the consumer. I ask why to help develop a series of hypotheses and then try to understand and use appropriate information sources and research techniques to generate meaningful insights before building these into the development of my product, promotions or brand plans. It is also a key part of my critical thinking, problem solving and strategic reasoning skills. Asking why is a hugely powerful technique that helps me identify strategic options and opportunities and evaluate them as well as identifying problems and potential solutions.

But how many of us have stopped asking why? How many of us are asked to do something by people we work with, or our bosses, and just write down the request, walk away and try to get on with it? We have no idea why we have been asked. We have had no opportunity to add value or improve the solution, because we don't know the problem. We just get asked (or told) what to do and we get on and do it.

I don't think my daughter would behave in this way. In fact, I know for certain she would not. If I ask her to do something, she almost always asks why. Or I if explain something to her, she asks why until either she understands or I can't actually explain it anymore because I don't actually know. At which point, I often change the question or retract my request.

I have found that the ability and willingness to ask why is actually lacking all the way up the management line. For example, the Managing Director has an idea which he briefs direct report A on who briefs direct report B who briefs direct report C and so on. By the time C, D, E or F get the brief, it is unclear and when they ask why, the briefer has absolutely no idea and gives the answer "because the boss asked for it". This is particularly unhelpful and de-motivational. What makes this situation worse is that when person F completes the task and the output is passed back up the ladder to the MD, it is almost always not on brief and he/she looks bad as a result. This is inefficient and annoying for all involved. If everyone down the ladder asked why, this situation would never arise.

On many occasions the briefing for any such project or task will fall into a meeting. Meetings are an important tool in communications and when they work they help us to get to know other people, build rapport and allow us to work as part of a team to solve problems, come up with ideas and make decisions. However, if they are badly planned, they can be a complete waste of time.

Whenever I have plans with Jolie, I make sure I have thought through what I want the activity to be like, what I need to take with, what I want others to have thought about prior to coming and how long it will all take. I also make sure that I have explained everything to Jolie. This is true of even the most simple activities like going to the park. For example, one Saturday afternoon, I explained that we were going to the park to meet her friend Mia. We were going to stay for one or two hours. I was going to take a drink and a snack with for both her and Mia and she could help me choose what to take. She was asked to get changed, go to the toilet and decide if she wanted to walk or ride her bike. Once we had left, there were no surprises, arguments or frustrations about why we were meeting at the park.

Within the workplace, one really useful tool to help people understand why you are meeting is the TRAP technique. It makes sure that you are clear on the time, resource, agenda and purpose required for a meeting. These elements should all be summarised when inviting someone to a meeting and also force you to make sure you are absolutely clear as to why the meeting is taking place. For each meeting include the following in your invitation:

Time: *explain the time expectation for the meeting (do you really need two hours?)*
Resource: *explain what information attendees should bring to the meeting, any preparation needed, who should chair the meeting and who should take the minutes.*
Agenda: *attach or detail out exactly what areas will be covered in the meeting, who is responsible and how your time allocated will be spent — this will give the chair a clear guideline to work to so the meeting doesn't overrun.*
Purpose: *the purpose/rationale of the meeting should outline why people are there, your meeting expectations and the intended outcome and next steps needed.*

A completed TRAP gives all invitees the opportunity to challenge why they have been invited, to send a more appropriate person, to invite others who may also need to attend or to add agenda items before the meeting starts. It ensures everyone understands the objectives, agenda & output expectations and makes the meeting more relevant and efficient.

In August 2011, it was my brother-in-law's wedding and Jolie was a bridesmaid. Elisa and I spent a long time ensuring we were prepared for the day and that Jolie was clear on what was going to happen. By the time the day came, she knew exactly what to expect and who was going to do what throughout the day. Mummy was going to have her hair and make-up done and then Daddy was taking them both to the bride's house at 1pm. There would be photographs and then we would all go to the ceremony where Jolie would have to walk down the aisle and then sit quietly for half an hour with grandma whilst Uncle Matt and Auntie Tanya were married. After the ceremony we would drive to the hotel for photographs and then we would have dinner and Jolie would be able to stay up very late at the party if she was a good girl. Every step was talked through so there were no surprises and Jolie knew exactly what to expect and who was doing what.

One of the techniques I use at work to replicate this understanding within a project management scenario is the RACI model. This is essentially a tool for assigning roles and responsibilities within a project team. There are four key roles that someone can be assigned:

Responsible – *the person doing the work to achieve the task.*

Accountable – *the person ultimately answerable for the completion of the task, the person from whom the 'responsible' is delegated the work and the person who has ultimate approval. There can only be one accountable per task.*

Consulted – *contributors whose opinions are sought with two-way communication.*

Informed – *people who are kept up to date on the progress of the task - often they are the recipients of this information once the task is complete via one-way communication.*

Each role should have just one RACI type so there is absolute clarity. When it is applied successfully, RACI has a number of benefits. It is a very visual way of differentiating and demonstrating everyone's role within the project. It clarifies what people are responsible for and where they share this responsibility. It makes clear who needs to be involved in which decisions and as only one person can be accountable for the completion of a task, the result is an increase in decision-making time. In short, RACI will help everyone involved in a project understand what they are meant to be doing to deliver it and why.

For the most part, I believe children are doers. Now don't get me wrong, they are by no means perfect. They often plan badly, rush into things without all the necessary thought and preparation and are pretty poor at finishing things and tidying up. However, when they have decided that they want to do something and they understand why, they want to do it immediately. As adults, we often find a great deal of excuses as to why we can't do something now or ever. I think if we could harness our inner child's desire to do and combine it with a more structured planning process, we would become the optimum project manager.

Chapter 5
Improving our attention

At times I truly believe that my daughter has the attention span of a goldfish (6 seconds I believe). If something doesn't interest her or if something else seems more interesting, she moves on quickly, generally leaving the first subject unfinished and probably in a mess. I see this behaviour in myself and colleagues all the time at work, especially when it comes to completing projects and tidying up loose ends and paperwork.

Occasionally, however, my daughter will find something that really captures her attention (when she was three, drawing or sticking) and whilst she is in the zone nothing can distract her. I have seen my wife become the stereotypical harassed mother trying to get Jolie to stop whatever she is doing and do something else. My daughter, like most children, can get so wrapped up in what she is doing that it takes a lot of persuasion (and sometimes bribery or threats) to make her do something else instead. This ability to focus totally on one thing comes naturally to us all when we are young but becomes more challenging as we get older. We have more distractions, we struggle to focus and concentrate and as a result, we fail to get on with the work we are meant to be doing.

Steve Jobs was famously quoted as saying "I'm as proud of the things we haven't done as the things we have done". This may sound surprising but he goes on to say that "People think focus means saying yes to the project or commitment that it has already been decided to focus against. But that's not what it means at all. It means saying no to the 100 other good ideas that there are. You have to pick carefully".

Achieving what Steve Jobs suggests is actually extremely difficult but I would suggest that at this stage we consider the importance of the 80:20 rule. Officially, this rule (also known as the Pareto Principle) argues that a small proportion of activity (i.e. 20%) generates an exponentially bigger return (i.e. 80%) and therefore we should concentrate on the activity likely to have the biggest impact. The reverse is that 80% of our time and effort only generates a 20% return. I personally believe that we can spin the 80:20 rule to mean that if a task is 80% correct, it is probably good enough and we should worry less about perfection and more about getting things done.

Even once we have chosen what tasks we need to complete, we still need to find ways of improving our focus and concentration in order to get in the zone and deliver them. When I started my job at SPAR, I spent a great deal of time making sure that I felt comfortable in my work environment. This led to a number of people making fun of me as I had lots of books and toys on my desk and pictures pinned up on the walls around me. I raided the stationery cupboard on day one and had a lot of fun choosing items from the stationery catalogue to make sure I could organise my desk in the right way. I asked for a new office chair that was of a higher quality and supported my back and I made sure that it was the right height for me to sit. I asked for a docking station, mouse, keyboard and screen for my laptop so that I didn't have to work from my laptop when at my desk. All of this may seem a little over the top but I am strong believer that being comfortable in my work environment plays a significant role in my ability to concentrate. The more comfortable I feel, the more likely I am to sit and focus.

Something else I do a lot at work is listen to music whilst working. For some people, if the music is too engaging then it can work against them and break their concentration. If this is the case then I would suggest trying instrumental music.

However, for me personally, listening to music helps me shut out other noise and distractions which helps me focus and concentrate better. I listen to music whenever I want to get something done, including on trains and in hotel business centres. I also try and control distractions by closing my email inbox, not answering my phone or working elsewhere, either at home, in a meeting room or at a coffee shop.

I would also suggest never to under-estimate the effect of food, drink and rest. As a parent, I am always conscious of how much my children are eating or drinking and am always striving to ensure they are well nourished. I also make sure they are well rested and if I want them to keep their energy levels up or if I think they are looking a bit tired then I adapt accordingly. Drinking and eating is vital as being de-hydrated or hungry will make it nearly impossible to concentrate. It is also important to get up and move around throughout the day, especially as studies have shown that regular walking can help increase your focus. To be really efficient, you can actually combine some of these tasks. For example, I take short breaks, generally to get a snack or a drink as this ensures that my brain gets a bit of a rest and I am also nourishing my body.

Once you are comfortable in your environment, you are rested and have ensured your body is well fed and watered, the only remaining challenge is your mindset. One of the other things that I do as a father is to feed Jolie in a certain order. I know what food she likes to eat the most, what she likes to eat less and what I want her to eat and I adapt the order in which I give her food to ensure we are both happy. My grandma used to do exactly this with my father. She would always give him his vegetables and meat first and only once he had eaten them was he able to have his potatoes (which he loved). When I feed Jolie, I ensure that she eats vegetables and meat before bread, potatoes or cous cous as she will always eat the latter, but if she eats it first she will claim she isn't hungry and won't eat the rest.

We can consider using a similar technique with ourselves or

our teams. I believe we should all have a balanced and mixed workload that includes work which we have to do and work we want to do. Some of our tasks should be within our comfort zone and others should push our boundaries. However, everyone's nature is to focus on the tasks they enjoy first and put off the things they like less until later or even to hope they might go away. Knowing this, and how we approach feeding a child, we can adapt to either only let them have more tasks in areas they like, once they have completed the tasks they like less or set them deadlines for both the areas at the same time to ensure all is completed. What happens more often than not, is that over time all the areas become liked (as they become known) and we have to push the boundaries once again.

With this in mind, I try and do the hardest tasks when I am most alert and full of energy and desire. I have to judge when this is for myself but generally I know if I am in the mood or not, and if not, there is little point in starting something that requires a great deal of focus and concentration. I do however, have a terrible habit of starting multiple jobs at the same time but I have realised that focusing on one task at a time, especially if it needs thought, is important. I try to switch between tasks that take a great deal of thought and others which are much lighter and require less attention and concentration to help balance the work throughout the day.

One of the things that can break our focus and concentration is people disrupting us. The most obvious way of managing disruptions is to talk to the person most likely to interrupt you. Working at home can be difficult, especially when Jolie is around because she constantly wants my attention. I have managed to avoid this problem (on some occasions) by talking to Jolie and setting boundaries. I explain to her that I have work to do and need 30 minutes to do it. I give her a drink, a snack and probably put on a DVD or TV programme and tell her that I will come and play with her soon. She is normally content for 30–45 minutes which allows me to get stuff done. At work, talking to someone who is likely to disrupt your work is key. If you have an office, try closing the door as this will generally stop people from casually stopping by as they will assume that if the door is closed you are busy. If you don't have an office, try wearing headphones. Often I put headphones in and forget to actually put on any music. People know when I am wearing headphones that I am trying to concentrate and if they do interrupt me, they are brief about what they require. The slow motion and disgruntled removal of the headphones to make the point that I am not happy being interrupted can also have great dramatic effect!

On the other side of the coin from staying focused is the ability to capture someone's attention. A few years ago I came across the term "inattentional blindness" which was coined by Arien Mack and Irvin Rock in 1992. It is a strange phenomenon that involves our mind ignoring events it is not concentrating or focusing on. This happens because we have a limited capacity for attention which limits the amount of information we can process at any particular time. This means if something is not processed by our attention, it will probably not be observed, even if it is within plain sight. In fact, the more difficult the task, the less likely we are to notice anything beyond it.

A variety of experiments have taken place to demonstrate this behaviour. Ultimately, we all make a common mistake believing that 'important' events will automatically draw our attention away from current tasks or goals. In reality, this is not usually the case. For example, I have lost count of the number of times that my wife has started talking to me about clothes she has just bought (or even tried on) when I am watching something (riveting) on TV. Days later I will see her in a new dress and comment on how nice it is and she will tell me that I saw it, she tried it on for me and I said I liked it. I have no recollection of this because I was focused on the TV when it all happened!

The best-known study demonstrating inattentional blindness

is the Invisible Gorilla test, which was conducted by Daniel Simons of the University of Illinois at Urbana-Champaign and Christopher Chabris of Harvard University. Their study involved subjects being asked to watch a short video of two teams passing a basketball in which one team was wearing black and the other was wearing white. The watchers were asked to count all the passes made by the team in black, both bounce passes and aerial passes. Mid-way through the video a person wearing a full gorilla costume wanders halfway across the screen, stops, bangs his chest and then walks across and off the screen the other side. When the video finishes everyone watching was asked how many passes they counted and if they noticed anything out of the ordinary take place. Amazingly over 50% of the people watching didn't notice the gorilla. I have run this exercise in many different companies as well as at home and for me an even higher percentage didn't notice. When I showed my parents the video again without asking them to concentrate and count the passes, they could not believe it was the same video as the gorilla was so obvious. Interestingly, in 2010 the video was remade into an advert on TV (with a moon-walking bear instead of a gorilla) designed to warn motorists about the danger of not noticing cyclists.

So how do we grab people's attention? How do we keep it once we have managed to grab it? Later in this book I take a look at influencing and persuasion skills that children naturally exhibit. However they are also brilliant at capturing and keeping our attention. Sometimes Jolie captures my attention in a rather abrupt and in-my-face way. She comes right up to me and pokes me whilst saying "Daddy" until eventually I give her my attention. Obviously, we can't do this at work but there are slightly more subtle ways of capturing someone's attention.

First there is whispering or talking quietly. Jolie does this all the time to us and vice versa for different reasons. From her perspective, it's normally to draw you straight into something secretive and intriguing (which probably turns out not to be!)

From a parent's perspective, whispering can work brilliantly when there is lots of noise and commotion (especially with lots of kids around). It works to calm the surroundings and draw people to you. Shouting can sometimes grab attention but if the environment is already too loud, then this will have little effect. However, whispering can often be more impactful because people go quiet and come close to listen to what you have to say. This can even work when presenting on stage to hundreds of people. If you are saying something particularly important, instead of getting louder in an attempt to drive your point home, try dropping your voice and confiding in your audience. You might be surprised that they will listen even more intently.

The pace at which you speak, the pitch, tone and the amount of pauses you choose to insert into your sentences can grab and hold attention. If you are able to change the pitch, stress and volume of your speaking voice as you talk to people you will be able to keep your audience (whether one person or five hundred) riveted. Of course, if you talk in a monotonous voice, you will sound boring and lose your audience very quickly. If you do feel that you are losing your audience, one trick that has worked for me is not to talk faster and louder but to actually just stop talking. It could be instant, it might take a few seconds and sometimes even a little longer, but the person who was listening will always apologise and then give you their full attention for you to finish whatever you were saying.

It is also really important to try not to make intrusive sounds like ums, ers, clicks of the tongue or little phrases that you probably don't even realise you are using like "you know", "I mean", "like" or "sort of". Linguistically these are known as fillers. One piece of feedback I received early in my career when presenting to a group of senior management was that I used the word "obviously" far too frequently. My manager at the time explained to me that whilst it was obvious to me because I had been living and breathing the project, it was not obvious to anyone else, even if they were more senior and experienced than I was. He wasn't suggesting that I detailed everything but that I ensured I gave enough information so that everyone was on the same page.

Making eye contact helps to demonstrate that you are engaged in the subject and that you are paying attention. Holding eye contact shows that you are interested and can help to display conviction, especially if you are the one speaking. People avoid making eye contact for a variety of reasons. They might be shy, anxious, shifty or too busy. One Sunday afternoon I was sorting some paperwork and my daughter was talking to me. She realised I wasn't paying attention and her solution was first to tell me to look at her and then to grab my head and force me to do so. I often walk into my boss's office and soon realise that he isn't paying attention to me. Whilst I can't walk over and grab his head to make sure he looks at me, I can stop talking until he looks up, makes eye contact and then carry on. Eye contact is a powerful and brilliant way of ensuring that you have someone's attention and that they are listening.

At times, children are utterly hilarious. Sometimes they mean to be and at other times they clearly don't! For example, I tore the ligaments in my ankle playing football and when I got home and limped into the house, Jolie said "What's wrong Daddy?" I told her I had hurt my ankle so she crouched down to take a closer look. "I can see. That's really bad. Poor Daddy" she said before standing up and asking me "Which ankle have you hurt?" The story may lose something when translated into text but it was funny and she had captured my attention and went on to tell me all sorts of things. Comedians on stage (or TV), especially the ones you find funny, are masters at grabbing your attention and holding onto it with humour.

It is also important never to underestimate the power of visual aids. How often do our children have a toy, a drawing or something else with them to help explain themselves. Visual aids are designed to enhance a presentation and keep the audience's attention, but it is important to realise that they are never a substitute for your power as a speaker. To me, ventriloquism is the absolute best example of someone who is able to capture and hold your attention, primarily using a visual aid (and humour) but no one is in doubt at any point (despite what it might look like) who is doing the speaking.

Finally and maybe the most obvious way of grabbing people's attention is to give them what they want. For adults this is probably in some way linked to time, money or energy and for children it could be as simple as a Fruit Shoot or as complicated as a trip to Disney World. The world of advertising is built on this point but the challenge is to truly understand what people want and this can be hugely difficult. With our children, we generally know because we spend a lot of time with them. With people we work closely with, we should know. And even when advertising, research should be able to generate the insights from which we develop and market a product. If Jolie is doing something and I want to get her attention, I have been known to wander past with some chocolate or an ice cream and it's amazing how quickly she sees what's going on!

Chapter 6
Negotiating like children

Someone once told me that "life is a series of negotiations". Since I have married and had children, this has become more and more apparent. My wife and I constantly negotiate, compromise and even occasionally argue. If, for instance, I leave her with both kids to play football on a Saturday morning, then she can leave me with both kids to go shopping on a Saturday afternoon. However, what I have noticed (especially since Jolie reached the age of two) is that there are undoubtedly negotiation skills that come naturally to a child that we as adults have lost. Even those of us who have been on negotiation training courses can struggle to replicate these skills as effectively.

On the most basic level, effective negotiation helps you to resolve situations where what you want conflicts with what someone else wants. It is simply the act of reaching agreement as to how to move forward and generally involves conceding in areas of lesser importance to gain in areas of greater importance. In every negotiation there are two key elements, what you want and what you really need. The former involves what we would ideally like to achieve (the wish list) and is probably our opening proposal. The latter defines what we absolutely must achieve, what concessions we are willing to make and what we definitely cannot trade. Somewhere in the middle is the negotiation zone, the area from which both parties will walk away content. The negotiation itself normally involves exploring the other party's position, proposing a solution, bargaining and closing.

If you believe that your dealings will be a one-off, then it may be possible to play hardball which involves seeking to win at the expense of the other person. However, with people you have to deal with constantly this style is not appropriate as one side always loses. A 'win-win' negotiation style should be the basis for all negotiations with people with whom you have an ongoing relationship. The aim is to find a solution that is acceptable to both parties, and leaves both parties feeling that they've won, in some way, when they walk away. This feeling is vital as it helps maintain good working relationships.

I once took Jolie to McDonalds for a Happy Meal. This was positioned as a treat for her but was also necessary as I was running late to feed her dinner. She was, of course, very excited. Once we had arrived and ordered, she spotted the soft play area. The negotiations began. She wanted to go in immediately whilst I wanted her to wait until she had eaten. I won by appeasing her with a balloon. She ate slowly and was wriggling around everywhere but the threat of not being able to play in soft play and taking away her balloon eventually got her to eat well enough. It all felt, as usual, unnecessary. After dinner she entered soft play and I knew I was going to struggle to get her out again. After 15 minutes I said it's time to leave. She refused and moved to the part of the soft play farthest away from the entrance. Five minutes later I resorted to saying goodbye, putting on my coat and hiding behind a pillar. I waited. A minute or so later she came out looking to see if I had really gone. I picked her up and we left. This entire experience was basically one long negotiation. I got Jolie to eat dinner and saved time, whilst she got McDonalds for dinner, a balloon, a toy and to play in soft play. It may have been a tiresome, long-winded process, but ultimately, Jolie and I both got something we wanted.

In virtually any situation, when a child asks for something and you say no, they refuse to take no for an answer. The traditional parent's response of "Because I said so", only gets us so far as they continually demand to know why. They stand their ground, continue to probe, challenge and are annoyingly persistent. Throughout this process we are slowly (or quickly!) worn down and our children gain the upper hand in a discussion that we didn't think was a negotiation but apparently it is and we are losing. Every negative response we provide drives them to be more creative and the more they listen and ask questions, the more power they gain. They use "What if?" questions, change the deal and broaden the negotiation beyond its original starting point to make the negotiation pie bigger rather than continue to fight over how to cut up the existing pie. They generally negotiate in a positive, enthusiastic and confident way using definitive language and by the end of the process, they have either got what they wanted or got something else instead or as well.

Whilst all these skills are extremely powerful, I want to pick out a few in particular. First it is very difficult to negotiate against someone who is enthusiastic and continues to change the basis of the negotiation. Ever since she was a baby, Jolie would normally be read three stories before bed. However, sometimes she would have done something naughty during the day and had a number of stories taken away as a punishment. When bedtime came the negotiations would begin. She would start by asking for all three stories. If she felt she wasn't going to get them she would offer to do her teeth nicely, promise to sleep till the morning, ask for one from memory with the lights off or ask for stories on her CD player whilst she went to sleep. More often than not the changing basis of the negotiation resulted in her getting all the stories she wanted, in one format or another.

Secondly, children use "What if?" questions naturally and effectively. These types of question are a step on from "Why" and are used to start and move negotiations on to a positive outcome. "What if I sit still in the shoe shop?" "What if I eat all my lunch?" "What if I sleep all night?" "What if I tidy up my bedroom?" Your instinct when reading these questions is probably that these are things the child should be doing anyway and I agree. However, how do you respond to the question? They are suggesting good behaviour and are hinting at a reward. We want them to behave well and are happy to reward them as such and, almost always, we offer them something for a behaviour they should and maybe would exhibit anyway. "If you sit still, I'll buy you an ice cream". "If you sleep all night, we can go to the park in the morning". I rarely use this style at work. "What if I complete this project on time?" "What if I work more hours than I should?" As managers we should be thinking how we can incentivise our team in this way and as employees we shouldn't be afraid to ask "What if…?" We could all end up in a more contented position.

One thing children do not lack is creativity. Like most children of her age, my daughter at three was extremely creative and could turn a sand pit into a beach or a climbing frame into an ice cream shop. This creativity was also used continuously throughout her negotiations. In April 2011, miraculously the weather was good so, of course, Jolie wanted to play in the garden all the time or go to the park. One day she asked if she could go into the garden. I said "No", mainly because I knew this would have involved me going into the garden, and I couldn't be bothered. She asked "Why?" I said "Because it is too cold". She said "But I will wear a coat" (and ran off to the cupboard to get her coat). I said "OK, but it is a little late and it's bath time soon". She responded with "But I'll only go out for a little bit and it's not bath time yet". I said, "But I don't want to go in the garden" and she retorted "That's ok, I'll go out by myself and you can come out if you feel like it". The result was that I had run out of excuses and she got to go in the garden.

Children are also brilliant at using high initial demands. This involves them starting the negotiation with a position that they know will be met by a "No" but is actually often not a position they care hugely about. Years ago, when my sister was a teenager she decided to ask our parents if she could have her belly button pierced. You can imagine the argument that ensued. They said "No" and so she started to cry and blame them for being controlling. She said that she would use her own money so they didn't need to worry. They refused point blank to allow this but conceded that she could have her ears pierced. She continued to argue and the outcome was that my parents agreed to take her to have her ears pierced, pay for it and even buy her first pair of earrings.

As I think back on how this argument unfolded, it occurs to me that before the argument (she instigated) she had never had any interest in having her belly button pierced but always wanted her ears pierced. She started with a high initial demand, knowing that my parents would refuse but hoping that she could negotiate what she really wanted. When I asked her about this later, she admitted that all she really wanted was to have her ears pierced and for them to pay for it. The earrings were a nice bonus!

At work, we could use this skill when negotiating with suppliers, colleagues or even our line managers. Start by asking for something which you are pretty sure you cannot get (but not ridiculously unrealistic) and see what they come back with. You will be surprised how often the result is an improvement on your current situation. A great example of this, used against me was when a member of my team asked for a meeting to discuss her future. She took me to Starbucks so we could chat openly and freely offsite and explained that she felt she had achieved all the objectives she had been set by her previous boss. She compared herself to other people across the business and demonstrated examples as to why she should be promoted and receive a pay rise. At the time, I had only been in my role for three weeks and so I was not in a position to meet all her demands. What we agreed was a set of objectives for the next three years with key milestones highlighted. If she achieved what we had agreed, then she would be promoted. At the end of the three year plan, she would have exceeded her peer group (both internally and externally) in terms of both position and pay. I also offered her a small but meaningful immediate pay rise to keep her happy and motivated. So even though her high initial demands weren't met, she improved her situation and was happy with the outcome.

What about throwing a tantrum? We have all experienced, either as parents or spectators, the wonder that is a full-blown child's tantrum. In fact my mum claims the only reason I was able to sit here and write this book is because my grandma stopped her leaving me in M&S when I was having a tantrum underneath the clothing racks at three years old (I have always hated shopping!) But surely this is a negative behaviour that shouldn't be replicated in the workplace? This was my first reaction but in reality, whilst people in the workplace do not generally lie on the floor kicking and screaming and having tantrums like children, many people do have tantrums in their own way. My uncle has been a very successful businessman for many years but is renowned for having fits of rage. Alex Ferguson, the Manchester United manager, has similar fiery traits to his reputation and is known to have thrown cups of tea and water bottles at his players. One of the girls who worked for me when I wrote this book would go silent and moody when she was 'having a tantrum' at work. In reality, our reaction to both the thought of these tantrums and the reality is to try to avoid them. However, with people we work for or those that work for us, they can't be avoided and as a result we often give in, especially if the things we are giving away are rationalised as 'little things'. In fact, we often give in before the negotiation has even happened. For example, when we know that if we do X, our boss will 'throw a tantrum', we inevitably try and avoid doing X in the first place. The trick could be to throw a couple of tantrums to demonstrate where the lines are drawn and then you will probably never need to throw one again! However, as managers we need to respond to this behaviour and develop our staff to prevent them throwing tantrums on a regular basis.

Children are also very skilled at asking the person they believe is most likely to agree to their request. They know which parent is likely to say yes to which question. They understand who is likely to be 'good cop' and who the 'bad cop' is. If they think that their parents might say no, then they will try and find a grandparent to ask instead. One summer, Jolie came into the kitchen and asked if I would fill up her watering can. I looked out the window and saw that she was going to water her sandpit and so I said "No". She shuffled off, head hanging low. A few minutes later I looked out the window to find her watering the sand pit. I quickly went out to find out if she was a genius who had managed to fill the watering can herself or whether someone else had helped her. Of course, her mother had filled the watering can. I then told Jolie that she could water the flowers but not the sand pit or I would take it away and she agreed. However, by finding the right parent, she got what she wanted. This is a technique that can be used easily within the work place. We normally have one direct manager who needs to approve certain things but if we need help with a project, we can certainly find someone else who is likely to help because (selfishly) they enjoy the type of work you are doing or they are passionate about the subject matter.

Building on this point is a child's ability to play parents off against each other. In our house, I normally agree something with Jolie (being the good cop that I am) and when Elisa later says no, she pipes up with "But daddy said I could". When Elisa then asks me, I have to support Jolie as I did say she could and thus Jolie wins. In many cases, Elisa had originally been asked and had already said no, but I wasn't aware of this. Children are also brilliant at using one parent to then fight their corner for them. Jolie will approach me and seed a thought in my head and I will then consider this, decide it's a good idea and then go to discuss with Elisa. We negotiate, agree and the winner is normally Jolie. To find people at work to fight our corner is always extremely powerful. There are many ways in which I have done this at work, from 'positioning' people before key meetings to asking someone else to raise a point on my behalf. The former helps to ensure that all concerns on a particular request have been dealt with before the meeting in question and therefore no hurdles or stumbling blocks arise when presenting (especially to senior management). The latter is a method where we get to play a supporting role as opposed to a lead role. If a board member suggests something, which we then support, there is often much more gravitas and a greater likelihood of a positive outcome.

Something that children have in abundance is patience and time. They are never in a rush. At a young age, they have absolutely no concept of time. Jolie always said "A long time ago" when she was talking about yesterday and "Soon" when she was referring to her birthday which was six months away.

Jolie also used the phrase "I'm just…" constantly to delay stopping whatever she was doing. In many situations, the fact that children take forever to do anything is actually a strong negotiation tactic. We probably start by threatening them with punishments and end up rewarding them for actually just doing what they were meant to do in the timeframe in which they were meant to do it. We can all use this technique really easily. The key thing to find out is the timeframe that the other party is working to and the influences on this timeframe. For example, a car dealership normally has targets to be met quarterly or yearly and if you can find out these timing pressures, it is sometimes easier to get a better deal as the sales person needs the sale to hit his targets and get his bonus. If a top executive flies into London to do a deal, find out when his return flight has been booked for and whether he has other meetings after yours which cannot be moved. If so, I would suggest taking your time in the early part of the meeting so that he/she is forced to concede some points later on in order to complete the deal in the timeframe they have available. When we bought our first house, we were in no rush but the family we were purchasing from had two children, were pregnant with a third and wanted to move before the baby was born. This meant that the longer we took and held out, the better the deal we got. We were careful however, not to take too long and lose the deal altogether and therefore once we reached a price we were happy with we agreed.

When you have an abundance of time, consider the technique of taking your toys and going home. In children, this can be a very negative behaviour but in business I would suggest that this involves controlling the timing, format and the presentation of information and discussions. Remember, you normally don't have to complete a negotiation in one go so if you can't reach a win-win position, then take a step back, go home and come back to negotiate another day. Obviously a slightly less extreme way of doing this is to take an adjournment. There are many times when this might be needed. You might feel that you have to reconsider your objectives in the light of changing circumstances. You might find out new important information which you need to factor in. You might need to consult your boss or your colleagues. You might just be in deadlock and need a break! It is important however, to note that before you take an adjournment, summarise the position the negotiation has reached and find a quiet and private area where you can discuss things freely with your colleagues. An adjournment creates an expectation that new information or proposals are going to be discussed, so you should never adjourn and come back to the same point as you will not be able to move forward.

The phrase 'rules are made to be broken' is often heard when someone is doing something they shouldn't be. Children are constantly pushing boundaries and breaking the rules. In some instances this is deliberate and in others less so but what is clear is that by ignoring the rules, they start in a strong negotiation position. If we take Jolie out to a restaurant and want her to sit still or stay quiet, we often have to start bribing her before we even get there. "If you sit still, stay quiet and eat your lunch, then we will..." When I was younger, I remember my mum taking me to the optician and promising that if I was a good boy, I would be taken to the sweet shop nearby and get a treat as a reward. If we change the rules at work, we can often put ourselves in a stronger negotiating position.

The response to the phrase "I love you daddy, you are the best daddy in the world" is most often "thanks Jolie. But what do you want?" And there is normally something (although not always immediately). Compliments can be a very powerful negotiating skill. Sometimes, we try and 'chat up' someone working in a hotel to get a room upgrade or at the EasyJet check-in counter so they won't notice or charge us for our excess baggage. We will say "Because you are so good at this, I wondered if you might be able to help me" when trying to convince colleagues to assist us. My boss once rewarded me for working beyond my standard requirements and doing a good job by paying for a meal for me and my wife. This was a great compliment and was hugely motivational. Never forget that being nice and complimentary to people goes a long way.

Chapter 7
Influencing and persuading

As well as being very good negotiators, children are very skilled at influencing and persuading their parents (and others). Influence and persuasion are employed in order to cause people to think, feel or do something that they wouldn't otherwise. Although we are all influenced in different ways, there are some key factors that affect us all. Whilst we believe that we listen to what people say and make decisions based on logic, a study from UCLA indicates that only around 7% of communication effectiveness is verbal whilst a massive 93% is non-verbal, and includes how we say something (the song) and how we move our bodies when we say it (the dance). How we say something incorporates the emphasis, speed, pitch and volume of our voice whilst our movement and body language involves our hands, posture, eyes and proximity. There are lots of ways children instinctively address these variables and by harnessing some of their simple and natural behaviours, we too can become stronger influencers.

One behaviour that most children exhibit with ease is the ability to find common ground. Many of us have probably thought how amazing it is that children immediately make friends, with almost no effort. For example, I took Jolie to the park one hot summer's day and within a few minutes she was playing in the sandpit with another little girl around six months younger than herself. They played together happily, having never previously met, just because they both had a bucket and spade. When I took Jolie to an athletics event, she played with a six-year-old girl, simply because they both liked running. In comparison, I went to a UKA (United Kingdom Athletics) sponsors' forum in which all co-sponsors of UKA spent an entire day together to discuss best practice and to generally network. Although we all had common ground in that we sponsored athletics, too many people brought their own agendas to the table and the result was that very little, if any, common work could be achieved. Children don't have an obvious agenda and this is something we can learn from. If the collective attitude that day had been "You sponsor athletics? I sponsor athletics - we're best friends", imagine the common projects that could have been agreed?

Children also have an amazing ability to forgive and forget. Whether this is with friends or family, it never takes long. One Saturday afternoon, Jolie had a friend round to play and after an hour or so of playing very nicely, they began to argue. This was because they both wanted to use the *Little Tikes* car. Could they agree to share or take it in turns? Of course not, they were three years old. There was shouting, crying, screaming and even throwing things. Eventually they calmed down (after some superb parenting of course) and they moved on to play with some bricks. This was only minutes after a huge falling out. Did either of them hold a grudge? Of course not. They had already forgiven and moved on.

I would suggest that for adults this behaviour is about 'being the bigger person' and I once experienced the perfect counter example at work. One of the women in my team was having an issue with an agency. I asked her what she thought she should do and I received a tirade of abuse regarding how useless this agency partner was and that they should be there to make her life easier. Having diffused this slightly, I asked the question again. After a few iterations she conceded that she needed to resolve the situation and the best way to do this was to air the issues and discuss them openly. I then asked if she would set up a meeting (or go for a drink) and I was told it shouldn't be her job. Now the reality is that whilst she was probably right, her attitude was helping no-one and the collective lack of respect meant that projects were starting to slip and her ability to influence, persuade or even work with this agency partner was suffering hugely. In the end, I encouraged her to be the bigger person and after a simple airing of issues, a new way of working was introduced and most of the issues disappeared. I accept that adults, by nature, are more complex than children and find it more difficult to just "get over" the baggage they carry. However, the point is that children don't generally make it personal. With Jolie it was never about her friend, it was about wanting the toy car. If we therefore approached work situations more like children and didn't make things personal, we would resolve any problems much more quickly.

Since Jolie turned three, she has become very effective at using non-verbal communication and her influencing skills continue to strengthen. She uses her body language to demonstrate whether she is happy, sad, annoyed, upset or excited and she uses her tone to emphasise what she is trying to say. For example, one Sunday morning, she walked slowly into the bathroom and said in a very quiet and soft voice whilst looking at the ground, that she had done something very bad. I asked what she had done and she took my hand and asked me to come and see. She walked slowly, keeping her head hanging low until we reached my study to discover that she had drawn on my desk because the pen had slipped off the paper. She then reached her arms up for a cuddle and apologised profusely. I immediately consoled and forgave her and almost instantly she ran off happy. If I had found the pen marks on my desk at a later point, without the benefit of an explanation, I would have been hugely annoyed. Yet because she managed the situation so well, I was influenced to console and only gently reprimand her.

To me this is a great example of when the song and dance of communication is used effectively. I am sure we have all witnessed the opposite on many occasions. For example, we see someone stand up on stage and say how happy and excited they are to be there but they say it in a monotonous low voice whilst looking at the floor. Being aware of the impact that our 'song and dance' can have when used effectively can have a major impact on our ability to influence other people. If you are trying to be assertive, then ensure that your movement and tone is designed to carry conviction without becoming aggressive. If on the other hand you are trying to be receptive, make sure you make the other person feel comfortable. Where children and adults both fail to influence and persuade is when their behaviour becomes either too aggressive or too passive.

This may help us understand why many people believe that you can never replace a face-to-face meeting with emails or even phone calls. With email, all we have to use is written words and the danger here is that the reader fills in the gaps and assumes a tone or a meaning that might not have been intended. I experienced this when I received what I thought was an aggressive and critical email and I responded accordingly. When I sat down with the sender to talk it through, it transpired that he did not actually mean it that way. The phone is slightly better as we are able to 'sing' using our words and our tone of voice but we aren't able to use body language. One thing I have always been mocked about is walking around whilst on the phone. However, I do this because I was told that if I move and gesture, then the meaning will come through in my tone of voice and this will help me to express myself more clearly. Obviously, in a face-to-face meeting we are able to utilise both our verbal and non-verbal communication skills to influence and persuade.

Children have no problem asking for what they want or need and then repeating their request again and again. For example when Jolie was about three and a half, she was obsessed with the TV programme *Everything's Rosie*. One morning, she said to me "I want to watch Rosie please". I said "You have watched nothing but Rosie for days, can't you watch something else?" She responded "Rosie is my favourite programme. I want to watch

Rosie". I offered her some alternatives and she said "I like all those programmes but this morning I want to watch Rosie". The result was of course that she got to watch Rosie. In a business context the key is to use the word 'I', be clear about what you want (without feeling the need to justify yourself) and to be a 'broken record' whilst showing that you have listened to the views of others. Now don't get me wrong, I am not advocating steam-rolling as often other people's ideas need to be taken into consideration and should sometimes be given preference over your own. However, this can be a powerful influencing technique, particularly when you are clear about your needs and you want action quickly.

Staying focused and repeating yourself can also be effective when trying to reach a decisive conclusion. One evening when Jolie was four, she was meant to be going to sleep but decided to get up and ask for water. I said "No" and so a debate ensued where she repeatedly asked for water until she wore me down and I did as she asked. The next day at work I was asking one of my team if she would help out another colleague. The responses kept coming with caveats, questions or conditions. I repeatedly asked the question, "Do you want me to tell Susan that you are happy to help her?" Eventually I received a "Yes" response and we moved on.

Children (especially younger ones) are almost always positive and enthusiastic. Their glass is half full and to them up is good and down is bad. Jerry Seinfeld (the comedian) captures this brilliantly on stage when talking about Halloween:

"Wait up you guys, I gotta fix it! Wait up! Wait up!' That's what kids say, they don't say wait, they say 'Wait up!' 'Cause when you are little, your life is up, the future is up, everything you want is up 'Wait up, hold up, shut up! Mum I'll clean up, let me stay up!' Parents of course, are the opposite. Everything is down; 'Calm down, slow down, come down here, sit down, put that down!"

There is no doubt that enthusiasm and positive energy is infectious and can be a hugely powerful influencing factor. It is inspiring and makes others feel good and more favourable towards you and what you are asking for. As adults, we can use this technique both in this simplistic form but also in terms of positive visioning, which involves positively thinking about the potential outcome of a situation. Every thought and emotion we experience sends a corresponding chemical reaction through our body via our nervous system. Positive thoughts will make us feel good because they release pleasurable chemicals and restore balance to the body. So imagine what it will be like when something works and you are more likely to achieve it. Our natural instinct is to focus on the negative possibilities and this makes them more likely to occur.

However, if we focus on something positive happening, that outcome becomes more likely. To do this, you will require imagination and honesty as you have to be true to yourself. Find somewhere you can relax and sit uninterrupted for a few minutes and imagine yourself succeeding in whatever situation is coming up. Picture how you will feel, what you will see, what you will say and what the other party will say. Then give yourself a few moments to live out the scenario in your mind.

I have been lucky enough to have enjoyed a number of talks from great sports coaches including Frank Dick. From 1979 to 1994 Frank was the British Athletics Federation's Director of Coaching and has since become renowned as one of the country's best and most inspiring motivational speakers. One thing that all these coaches talk about at some stage is what makes people "Winners". Frank Dick says that "Winners are people of vision. They are dreamers who constantly visualise achievement and success whilst asking themselves 'What if?' They have and use imagination to anticipate and create change". The writer George Bernard Shaw was famously quoted as saying: "Some men see things as they really are and ask 'why?' I dream of things that never were and ask 'why not?' Miles Hilton Barber, a blind adventurer, says

"All achievers are dreamers but not all dreamers are achievers". Children have fantastic imaginations and are hugely creative and if we can harness some of this creativity and combine it with positive visioning, we can achieve so much.

So far, I have looked at a number of behaviours that Jolie uses to influence me, but there are also some behaviours that I use as a parent which help me to influence Jolie. I started to use these behaviours at work as well and they proved effective. First, is ensuring that Jolie or the other party is part of the decision-making process and ideally that they feel the decision is their own. For example, when giving Jolie lunch or dinner, I often ask her what she wants to eat as I have found that if she is part of the decision, she is much more likely to actually eat. What I do not ask her is if she is hungry or wants dinner as I would not get the answers I want. At work, I use a similar technique when asking people how they would approach a specific task. This bypasses needing to ask them if they want to approach the task and takes them forward quickly towards finding a solution.

However, I have learned over time that this doesn't necessarily mean giving the other party full control of the decision from start to finish, but just enough to engage and motivate them. For example, when giving Jolie dinner there are times when I don't actually want to give her a completely free choice and therefore I will give her some decision-making capability and flexibility, but within a controlled environment. So I will ask her if she wants spaghetti or whirly whirly pasta, fish fingers or chicken nuggets or sausages with peas or beans. At work I often use this technique, especially when asking management for a decision. I have found that if I take them one clear recommendation with no other options, they desperately try and find a way of 'adding value' which generally involves asking for something that isn't there, normally delaying and complicating the process. If on the other hand I take two or three options, any of which I would be satisfied to go ahead with, they feel like they have added value and been responsible for the decision themselves and I am happy as things are now able to progress. Framing decisions in this way is only scratching the surface of behavioural economics and the psychology of choice but is certainly impactful.

I also use the concept of silent allies at home and at work. This stems from the belief that people are more likely to do something if other people have already done it. In a sense, it fits perfectly with the old analogy that people 'never eat in an empty restaurant'. My wife always used to encourage Jolie to eat certain food by saying things like "But Mickey Mouse eats pasta". At work, I compare my team to others across the company or to myself, in order to influence them to do or behave in the way I believe they should.

As I have demonstrated, influencing and persuading people to do something can involve a variety of methods. The setting may be a one-on-one with your child or a colleague or it could involve presenting on stage to 500 people. Underneath it all, the skills required to achieve a successful outcome are the same. You have to understand your audience, prepare your content and deliver it confidently.

It is also worth thinking about your audience's attention span. Using headlines and grouping information into bite size chunks will make it easier for anyone to absorb and understand. When we talk to our children we try to remove all jargon and explain things simply and effectively. We have to remember that at work, whilst we live and breathe our topics, many of the people we are trying to influence and persuade do not and it is vital that they understand what we are trying to say if they are going to buy into it.

A few years ago, when I worked for General Mills, I recall a very senior executive coming to present to the company. He was second or third in command of General Mills in the USA and he was undoubtedly one of the finest speakers I have ever heard. He flew into Heathrow airport, jumped in a taxi and drove straight to our offices. When he arrived, he walked into the boardroom where all the staff had gathered, walked to the front, and started speaking. Even years later I recall *how* he delivered his address and the fact that he started by laying out what he was going to tell us, then he delivered his presentation and finally he summarised what he had told us. Everyone was completely clear on the message this man wanted to deliver. I do something similar with Jolie all the time. If we are going somewhere or doing something that we haven't done before, I will always tell her what I am going to tell her, tell her in detail and then summarise and get her to repeat back to me to see if she has listened and understood. Normally, I do this because I want her to behave and sometimes it actually works!

What about story telling? As a parent I do this all the time, whether reading from books, telling Jolie something that happened today or when I was younger by making up an imaginary story for creative play. Story telling is probably the most powerful tool that exists for engaging members of an audience, however small or large, and once we have engaged them, influencing and persuading them becomes much easier. I originally wrote this chapter just after a SPAR National Sales Conference where Miles Hilton Barber was the motivational speaker. For those of you who have never heard of Miles, he went blind at 21 but has since gone on to challenge barriers, seek adventure and succeed on expeditions to deserts, mountains and Polar Regions. He is an inspirational man who lost his sight but found his way. Because Miles' story is so powerful, we decided to shuffle the conference running order so that he could go first. He led the audience on a journey which resulted in them accepting they should try new things and believing they could tackle any challenge. We then kept the audience on that journey for the rest of the conference. Our feedback forms indicated that it worked a treat! Stories are powerful and inspiring. Finding a relevant way to harness and apply this at work could be the most powerful influencing skill of all.

Chapter 8
Dealing with fear and change

At three and a half, Jolie had perfected the art of walking and so she decided that she didn't need to hold my hand anymore. As a result she was forced to wear reins. Why? Because she kept running into the road. She had no fear and whilst sometimes this could be a benefit, at times, this became a problem. As parents, we instil fear into our children. Fear of getting hurt. Fear of the unknown. Fear of crowds. Fear of falling. Fear of strangers. Then once we have taught them fear, and they exhibit it, we get annoyed when they demonstrate fear in a situation where we think they are being 'silly'. It's a no-win situation.

Perhaps we use fear as a way of controlling our children. Sometimes it seems like the only way. I have heard parents say "The monster in the cupboard will get you if you get out of bed" or "God will punish you if you answer back". When our children are too young to understand that running into the road is dangerous, we try and scare them into behaving the way we would like. This clearly didn't work with Jolie and the result was that, for a period of time, we had to tie her to our wrists. A little later, my wife taught her a song about crossing the road that she had learnt in her own childhood:

Stop, look and listen, before you cross the street.
Stop, look and listen before you cross the street.
Use your eyes and your ears, before you use your feet
So stop look and listen, before you cross the street.

Jolie started to sing this when we went out and actually told me off for stepping into the road. She told me that it was dangerous, I might be hit by a car and that she would really miss me if I died! Then she started to teach the song to me.

The challenge for parents is to find a way of protecting their children without instilling fear. Jolie's nursery school teachers told me that to achieve this we should be positive in our phraseology when talking to her or Fraser. In the same way that someone shouting "Don't look down" when you are on a bridge almost always makes you look down, if we immediately give a fearful message to our children we are actually making the situation more dangerous and increasing the likelihood that what we are warning against will actually occur. So, instead of shouting to a child "That's dangerous", "Be careful" or "Please don't fall", we should instead be telling them to "Use their steady feet" (and subtly and calmly going to help them). Instead of asking "What's that?" in a drawing they have created, we should ask them to tell us about it. Using positive phrases is likely to encourage them as opposed to using negative phrases, which can scare them. We can take this learning into the workplace and try to be more positive and encouraging with our teams and colleagues. I think in most cases, it is actually us, as parents or bosses, who are afraid.

Fear driving tactics are frequently used in advertising, especially in public safety announcements, for example to raise awareness of the need to wear a seatbelt, the effects of drink driving or as a fundraising appeal for children's charities. The majority if not all of this advertising is shock and scare-oriented. They generally involve some form of slow motion action where someone is badly injured, blood flies everywhere, people look ashamed and sorry for what they have done and we as the audience are left, in theory, so scared by what we have seen that we would never behave in such a stupid manner. The reality is that whilst this advertising is full of impact, it does not always connect with the viewer in the way that it could.

In contrast, advertising aimed at children is always positive, playful and designed to show how great a toy is, whilst generally in a setting that the child can relate to. Of course the two are very different subject matters but at their heart, one is connecting with the audience in a negative manner and the other in a positive one.

I was lucky to be shown a fantastic seatbelt advert from South Africa in 2011 which takes this latter principle and puts it into action. The advert involves a father sitting in a chair in his living room 'driving' towards his wife and daughter who are seated on the sofa. As the advert continues, and the poignant music plays, the father glances left, looks towards his family with fear in his eyes and steers the imaginary wheel away from some form of danger. At this point his wife and daughter slowly get up, cross the room and lock their arms around him in the form of a human seatbelt (and a hug). The film speeds up as he 'crashes' and glitter flies everywhere but he is perfectly safe in the arms of his family. The line comes up at the end: "Embrace life; wear a seatbelt". This connects so strongly with me as a parent as the thought of an accident causing my wife to be without a husband or my children to be without a father is far scarier than the fear of physical injury.

I have personally suffered from fear and anxiety. I have been to hypnotherapy and actually read the book *Feel the Fear and Do It Anyway* by Susan Jeffers in an attempt to conquer it. Whilst some of the techniques in this book are a bit extreme for me personally, learning that other people have fears and concerns was actually a real comfort. The book's basic premise is that your aim should not be to get rid of your fears. You should feel your fear, but not let it stop you from doing things you really want to do. I have tried to really embrace this principle.

One of my fears was presenting to large groups of people. For some reason I became really nervous, couldn't eat and dreaded every second, until I stood up, and then I actually enjoyed it. The turning point was someone asking me how I felt when other people presented. I realised that I didn't want them to fail, forget their words, sound stupid or look bad. I actually wanted them to present really well. I realised that most people would feel the same way about me presenting and that feeling of positivity has helped me present to a wide variety of audience, including one of over 400 people.

One of the most common fears that I have observed is the fear of change. Yet what I find curious is how young children all seem much more accepting of change than adults. For example, when Jolie was two years old we decided to move house. It was not the smoothest of processes. We sold our house in March 2009 with a delayed six-month completion. Unfortunately, when the six-months were up, we still hadn't managed to buy a new house and we moved into my sister's flat for three months before finally moving into our new home. Then after another three months we moved out into my parents' house for seven weeks whilst we had some building work carried out. For my wife and I, this process was hugely unsettling and repeatedly we had to find a new routine to make things feel normal. For Jolie, however, it was all fairly easy. She adapted to each situation easily and dealt with the ambiguity and change with very little effort and no anxiety or fear.

Dealing with change at work can be particularly tough. A new boss, a new office or a new job can all be scary experiences. The blind adventurer, Miles Hilton Barber says "If you can change it, why worry? If you can't change it, why worry?" However this philosophy can be tricky to adopt, especially as everyone deals with change differently.

One of my favourite books on this subject is *Who Moved my Cheese?* It is a simple, intriguing tale about dealing with change. The cheese is a metaphor for whatever is important to you in your life and the story involves two 'little people' and two mice who live in a maze. The question the book poses is how long will we wait for someone to bring us more cheese before we realise that it isn't coming and we have to venture out ourselves to find new cheese to eat.

Every time I have moved jobs, I have been afraid. Would

the grass be greener somewhere else or was it better the devil I know? In virtually every instance I waited too long to move but eventually I chose to seek out new opportunities. There was always a tipping point where I realised that I wasn't going to get what I needed (or had been promised) and I would either have to change my goals or move roles to achieve them. I was careful never to wait until I was really unhappy and desperate to leave as this enabled me to take my time and choose my next position carefully. Fortunately, each move has been beneficial and I have learnt that sometimes we have to be brave and accept the need to change to move forwards.

By trying to teach our children to be careful when crossing the road or jumping off furniture we bring fear into their world. As a result they start to look at the potential negatives in many situations. What I noticed as Jolie got older was that she became more fearful. Sometimes these fears were genuine and rational whilst at other times they were imaginary. As a father, I realised that helping Jolie overcome fears eased her personal anxiety but also built trust and strengthened our relationship as she saw me as a strong source of support. These feelings and benefits come from helping anyone cope with or conquer their fears, including our teams at work.

The first thing we need to understand is what they are afraid of and why they are afraid. I once read that children don't think like adults because at a young age (particularly two to four years old) they develop the ability to imagine monsters but don't have the ability to reason them away. I personally don't think this problem is limited to children. Whilst I don't imagine monsters, I do have irrational fears that I can't reason away. We can be too quick to assume that because we have developed logical reasoning as adults, we can rationally talk our way out of any fears and concerns but we certainly cannot. If we can understand both what we are afraid of and why we are afraid, then we can conquer our fears.

As parents we naturally behave in a number of ways that are designed to help our children cope with their fears. As with many other subjects I have looked at in this book, we ourselves do not then exhibit them at work. The first thing that my wife and I do as parents is encourage our children to share their fears. We want them to trust us enough to be willing to tell us what troubles them and allow us to try and help them deal with it. We are always sympathetic and make sure that we don't try and make them feel that it's wrong to be afraid. We acknowledge their fears, sympathise and empathise without reinforcing them. We try to find the balance between ignoring their fears and getting too sucked in (because children are cunning and can use some 'fears' as a way of not going to bed!) In a similar way, at work, I have learnt to encourage my team to share their fears as this can take away a lot of their scariness.

We try to hide our own fears to make our children brave. If we are scared of spiders or dogs, we have to try as parents to hide these fears, be brave and deal with situations so that our children do not pick up our fears. In some instances having to be brave for our children can help us in our own lives. For example, I have never been a fan of heights but when Jolie was young I had to conquer my fears in order to teach her how to use some of the high bars and nets in the playground. When shortly after I had to do a high ropes course on a friend's stag do, I was no longer afraid. At work, we have to show our teams that we are not afraid in order to give them the confidence to try new things. For example, if they know we don't want to present, they will not want to either. If we actively avoid certain meetings, they will try to do the same.

In instances where we aren't afraid, or we have outgrown our fear, this is really easy. I can say to Jolie, "It's ok to be afraid of the dark. Daddy used to be afraid" and help her by putting on a night light. I can do this because I am no longer afraid of the dark. But what about when we are afraid? My wife is scared of spiders and if she is on her own, or just with me, she will often freak out. However, if Jolie is around she will try really hard to hide her fears so that Jolie doesn't pick them up herself. We have to be brave for our children and try to lead by example. Our children watch us and if we do something and it is safe for us, they will assume it is safe for them. At work, we often hide behind others and behave very differently. I once saw a Director hide during a conference because the three-minute energiser involved catching a beach ball and saying one word out loud to the room. This then meant that his entire table tried to avoid getting involved. On the flip side I watched the film *Invictus* where Nelson Mandela, in his first term as the South African President enlists the national rugby team on a mission to win the 1995 Rugby World Cup in an attempt to unite the apartheid-torn country. It was clear that Captain François Pienaar's attitude towards fear helped drive his team to victory in the Rugby World Cup. The underlying point is that we need to lead by example. We do this as parents and often talk about it in the work place but do we really do it?

As parents we encourage our children to tackle their fears by gradually increasing their exposure to them over time. For example, when Jolie found out that she had to go to the doctor to have her jabs, she was afraid. She had hated the experience the first time and was afraid to go back. To help combat this, we bought her a Peppa Pig doctor's kit so she could give injections to her toys. When we went to the doctors, she was absolutely fine. When Fraser was younger, like many children, he developed separation anxiety, and would cry if Elisa or I left him. This started to affect how he slept and how he ate. The solution was to gradually leave him more and more, either in his play pen or with friends or family. At first we only left him for short periods and would check on him every few minutes (whilst trying not to be seen) and after a while he learned that he didn't need us around the whole time and got over it. At work we can help our staff conquer their fears in a similar way. For example, when a member of my team was reluctant to speak publicly, I ensured that I gave her opportunities to do so in an unpressured environment and to a limited audience until she became comfortable. Then when she had to speak to a larger audience, she was much less afraid.

We often reward Jolie or Fraser for dealing with their fears. This demonstrates a recognition that we understand that they have been brave, dealt with a difficult situation and that we are proud of them. When I was younger, if I was brave and well behaved when my mum took me to the dentist, I was allowed to visit the toy shop next door and buy a small gift. After a while, I wasn't afraid to go any more and didn't need any rewards. I would encourage you to reward yourself and your teams at work for successfully dealing with daunting situations.

I believe Jolie and Fraser have probably learned more throughout their lives from the things that have gone wrong than the things that have gone right. I know this is true for me. In a strange way, we need pain, regret, guilt or embarrassment to drive us to improve. If Jolie falls off the balance beam, she gets back up and tries again until she masters it. If Fraser closes his fingers in the toy box, he will know not to do it again. If I mess up a presentation or a project, I need to figure out why and change for the future. We must try to be less fearful of making mistakes as they can teach us a great deal. At work, I make a point of reviewing every project with my team to ensure that any learning is captured and acted upon.

We also teach our children that perfection is nearly impossible to achieve. We should not and cannot expect perfection or we are pushing ourselves towards anxiety, fear and failure before we have even started. My wife once even burst our in tears because she forgot to take something out of the freezer for dinner and decided she was a failure as a mother and a wife. Life is a jumbled mess full of bad days and things not going to plan and if we embrace this fact we can adapt and cope with all the stresses that life brings. However, if we aim for perfection, even on small things, we are setting unrealistic expectations and driving stress into our lives.

I have seen fear defined as Fake Evidence Appearing Real and learnt first hand that avoiding fears can actually make them scarier. If you face whatever you are afraid of, the fear will start to fade and become easier to cope with until eventually it is no longer a problem and you are not afraid anymore. Eleanor Roosevelt once said "You gain strength, courage and confidence by every experience in which you really stop to look fear in the face. You must do the thing you think you cannot do". I would encourage you all to consider that an admission of fear is not a time to show cowardice but an opportunity to show courage.

Chapter 9
Listening is caring

Sometimes at work it feels like unnecessarily hard work to have to deal with people and their complicated emotional needs. And it feels very difficult to put them first. Surely they are being paid to do a job and they should just come in and do it? Any baggage that they have from home should be left at the door or hidden deep so I don't have to see it or hear about it. I don't need to deal with their problems, why should I care?

I am sure at times that we all feel like this. Sometimes, we have our own problems outside of work and we don't want to deal with someone else's at work. But we have to. We have to remember that people at their core can't always separate home and work life. The common link between work and home is you. More often than not, if you leave home in a bad mood, you will arrive at work in a bad mood. If you are boring at work, you will probably be boring at home. If Jolie has a bad day at nursery, or is just tired and ratty, we have to deal with this behaviour at home. Realising and remembering this is vital when managing people as if we just ignore the problem and hope it will go away, it will probably get worse.

Children often make these situations easier to deal with because they volunteer to tell us what is wrong. When they are really young this is through crying. If they are hungry, tired, thirsty, in pain or need a nappy change, they cry. Amazingly, as parents we actually learn to understand what the crying means and we are able to distinguish between the different sounds. As they get older, although crying remains a fairly important part of their repertoire, they are able to articulate what the problem is. If we want to find out more, we often ask their friends, family or teachers to help us gain an insight into the real problem so we can then work it through with them. Sometimes the closest I come to this at work is by asking someone "What's Rebecca's problem today?" This is clearly not that supportive or caring!

To help build a trusting relationship, it is vital to understand how people are feeling and why. However, this can be extremely difficult. With our teams at work, it is sometimes hard to recognise if someone is having an issue and even harder to recognise the reasons why. It could be driven by work or home. It could be project based, people based or even health related. The solution is to talk about it. If you can make them aware that you care about how they feel, they are more likely to perform better at work as a result. I always try and ask my team (in a slightly cheesy way) on a scale of one to ten how happy they are and on a scale of one to ten how busy they are. Whilst this is often mocked, after a couple of questions to follow up, it becomes apparent if one of them is too busy or bored, unhappy or happy and then I can try and uncover the reasons why and if or how I can help. If the problem is work related, then I can always help. If the issue is home related, I can normally help in ways I didn't expect. It might be that they just need to talk about an issue out loud or it might be that they need to take a few hours at home to work things through and if as their manager I can facilitate this, they will be far more motivated and it will enhance our relationship.

We can start to understand why emotional connections are so powerful by looking at neuroscience and the human brain. My simplistic understanding is that the human brain has three key parts, or layers, which control how the brain processes information and makes decisions. The primitive part (the spinal cord and base of the brain) is responsible for many of our automatic systems and is core to our survival. Breathing, eating and sex all fall to this part of the brain. Around this is the emotional layer (the limbic system) where fear, happiness and aggression all start to play a part. Finally, surrounding and encasing this is the rational part of the brain (the human cortex). It manages a variety of things including logical reasoning, abstract thinking, hearing, seeing and our personalities. This is called the 'executive' part of the brain because, when we allow it, it considers all the inputs from the brain and makes rational decisions.

According to scientists who have studied and photographed the brain when it is making decisions, whilst all three parts are active, the rational and emotional parts are constantly in conflict and it is not always logic that governs. Often our emotions win over rationality and we then create logical explanations afterwards. These interactions occur deep within our brains so quickly that we aren't even aware of them.

I think this is really interesting and powerful when we consider building relationships with others. When we connect emotionally with others, we build a much stronger and deeper rooted bond and actually care about how they are and how they are doing. If we have any form of friendship with a colleague we are much more likely to try and help them than if we don't know them at all. We tend to answer the phone to people we know and like and ignore those we don't. I once had a very transactional relationship with a colleague until we enjoyed watching a football match together. After that point we got on really well, were pleased to see each other, and helped each other at work a great deal. The difference between before and after was a stronger personal connection. It is vital that even at work we build trusting personal relationships which go beyond the transactional nature of everyday working life.

With our children, we have an extremely strong and deep bond, but this is rarely replicated at work. I would suggest that one of the reasons we have such a strong bond with our children is that we understand what they want and need (most of the time) because we actually listen and really hear what they say.

Listening is simply the art of focusing on hearing someone. However, listening and hearing are very different skills. The first degree of listening is where we are actually not listening and as a result we hear nothing. One step up is when we are vaguely listening and only really trying to pick out information that is relevant to us. If we are more engaged, we probably hear everything being said but we don't necessarily go deeper to understand why it is being said. If we are fully engaged we will hear all the content and words as well as the signals given off by their body language and tone and we truly hear them.

Everyone wants to be heard. When we listen to others we confirm their need to be appreciated and understood. Deep down inside we all want to feel that we are important and know that we matter. We want others to listen to us when we are speaking and if someone does listen to us, we usually take an instant liking to them. Now I'm not suggesting that we should pretend to be interested with the aim of being liked. I am suggesting that if we improved our listening skills, we would fuel our social, emotional and professional success in the same way that a parent listening to their child helps to build his or her self-esteem. In the business world, listening can save time and money by preventing misunderstandings and driving greater cooperation. It is important to remember that we can always learn more when we listen than when we talk.

There are lots of reasons why we don't listen, including distraction, boredom, busy minds, lack of interest, lack of understanding, short attention spans or we might have heard it all before. We might just be too caught up in ourselves or it could be that the person talking is not engaging us. I used to get told off by my team at work all the time for not really listening. I used to ask someone on a Friday what they had planned for the weekend, they told me, I wished them well and then on Monday I asked them what they did. This just implied that I didn't listen to them at all on Friday, annoyed them and made them feel unvalued. I now try very hard to listen and remember the answers to questions I ask.

Jolie like all children and adults will hear the familiar sounds around her. She will hear her little brother crying, the oven beeping, the fish tank bubbling and the washing machine spinning but just because she has heard these sounds, doesn't mean they have actually registered in her brain. I was once told that teaching Jolie listening skills would be one of the most important things that I could do for her as a parent. I was also told that reading to her is a great way of developing her listening skills. Sometimes it feels like the only time Jolie listens is when I am reading her bedtime stories. I know she is engaged because when I try to skip pages, paragraphs or change the words to the story, she corrects me. We even created a game where I would state lines from one of her books and she would have to name the book. She would get it right every time proving she not only listened but engaged and remembered.

Jolie will often copy what I am doing when I am telling her something. When looking into listening skills in more detail I discovered that this is actually a skill called mirroring which involves mimicking the other person's facial expressions and body positions. When Fraser was very little, I would make distinct faces to gauge his reactions. If I made a sad face, he would start to get upset. If I smiled, he would smile. If I laughed, he would laugh. Our physiology, particularly our facial expressions, gestures and posture can affect how we feel and mirroring can actually help us gain a deeper understanding of what the person speaking is saying by allowing us to feel what they are feeling.

Jolie naturally uses her body language to let me know that she is paying attention and cares about what I am saying. She makes eye contact smile, laughs, acknowledges what I am saying ("Uh-huh" or "Yes daddy") and of course asks probing questions. These skills ensure that she appears engaged, focused and allows her to ask questions to clarify her understanding. To make sure she has listened and understood, I will often ask her some questions, and get her to repeat back to me some key pieces of information and sometimes I even ask her to summarise what she has heard.

Whilst I was working hard to develop Jolie's listening skills, I realised how much I struggled when it came to remembering people's names, especially if introduced at a party or gathering. I never used to listen to their introduction but as the conversation progressed I started to listen to what they said and later I realised that I could tell you where they went to school, where they lived and the name of their dog but not their actual name. My wife was aware of this trait of mine and understood that if she came over and I didn't introduce her immediately it was because I couldn't remember who I was talking to. She would then introduce herself, repeat back their name and how they knew me and I would apologise for being so rude for not introducing her. I have since got much better in this area and one trick I was taught was to use the person's name three times early in the conversation to embed their name in your mind.

Because I care deeply for Jolie, I truly focus on what she is saying and as such, not on myself. As parents we naturally want to hear what our children want to say but at work we have to force ourselves to be listeners. It is often tricky to stay focused when people are talking as we have lots of thoughts running through our heads. We might be hungry, tired, planning our evening or we might just be thinking about what we want to say next. We might even think we know what the person is going to say, but we might be wrong. Whilst difficult, it is vital to give the speaker your full attention, to be genuinely interested in them and what they have to say. If you feel your mind wandering, change the position of your body and try to concentrate on the speaker's words. Try and listen for main ideas. These are generally the most important points the speaker wants to get across. They may be mentioned at the start or end of a talk, and repeated a number of times. Pay special attention to statements that begin with phrases suchas "My point is" or "The thing to remember is".

It is also important not to judge the speaker or try to develop counter arguments when they are speaking. You should let the speaker finish their thoughts before you respond with what you want to say. If you do have something to say, hold it, nod and restrain yourself from jumping in. Speakers appreciate having the chance to say everything they would like to say without being interrupted. When you interrupt, it looks like you aren't listening, even if you really are. Once you have let the speaker finish, take a second to pause before responding to let yourself finish listening before you begin speaking.

Without delving deeply into selfish genes, kin selection and reciprocal altruism, it's obvious that we are hard wired to listen to and help our children, siblings and other relatives, all of whom we share common genes with. We are not programmed, however, to have the same empathy or feelings towards our colleagues. Whilst this can make listening more difficult, it also means that we don't care as deeply for our teams, colleagues or staff as we do for our family or closest friends. You might be thinking 'of course not'. But when you think about this further, whilst I wouldn't love them to the same degree as my son or daughter, I should truly care about them and their achievements. Otherwise, how can I ever hope to get the most out of them? And how can I ever be a good manager?

Over the years I have noticed how often management takes credit for the work of their staff, whether implied or by directly stealing it. I once saw a colleague present some work to the Board, which I knew for a fact was written by one of his team. He did not give them any credit, in either written form or when talking through the work. In essence, he took credit for someone else's work. At university or school, this would have been classified as plagiarism and cheating. At work, this was apparently acceptable behaviour. I too have been guilty of similar acts. Early in my career, I wanted to take as much credit as possible for everything to further my own status. I experienced my boss 'stealing' credit on many occasions, yet when I found myself in a management position, I started to behave in the same way. I would come up with many reasons why I did this including the fact it wasn't appropriate for my team to present to the board, it might not be good enough, it might look like I wasn't doing my job properly and so on. This actually makes no sense as the better the information provided by my team, the better they look and the better I look for managing them well and getting the best out of them. Nowadays, I try to always give credit where it is due and to actually go one step further and help them build their profile by presenting their own work to senior management as often as possible.

Now imagine if this was one of your children. Could you ever imagine stealing credit for work they had done? Could you ever imagine pretending something they had written was actually written by you? Of course not. Whilst this could be because our children's "work" is not considered competition, the behaviours are at opposite ends of the spectrum. As parents, we want to show off and exhibit all of our children's exploits, even when some of them are pretty poor and our friends politely say "Very nice". I truly believe that we should be proud of the achievements of our staff in the same way. In some cases this may even be because we had a hand in their success.

Once there has been success, we must try to celebrate it. The birth of a new child is reason enough to celebrate and at home this trend continues from that point onwards. Naming the baby, good school reports, birthdays, qualifications, degrees, marriage and so on are all celebrated with friends and family. At work, success is generally rewarded with a "Well done" and working life continues. At General Mills when we had successfully presented our business plans to the board, my boss took our whole team out for a meal and some drinks to celebrate. This brought everyone together, allowed us all to enjoy that moment of success and motivated us to strive even harder for success in the future. With our children we are encouraging, supportive, motivating and proud. With our staff we should endeavour to be the same.

Chapter 10
Who is really in charge?

As an adult, I like to believe that I am the one in control of my destiny, my wife, my children, my staff, my life! But I think much of the time I am not actually in charge of anything. At work I am told what to do by my boss and upwardly managed by my team. At home I am told what to do by my wife, my daughter and to an extent my mum and mother -in-law. Am I ever really in charge? I am sure sometimes I am, surely I must be?

In May 2011, Fraser was five months old and Jolie was three and a half. It was a difficult month as I was finding it hard to get Jolie to do what I wanted at home and one of my team to do what she was asked at work. In both scenarios, people were rebelling, challenging, being 'naughty', not doing what they were meant to and at times being hugely disrespectful. Could I be a boss and a friend? A father and a friend? Can both parents be strong or does one always have to be the good cop? What happens when the roles and boundaries all blur? Are they better at negotiating, influencing or persuading than I am? These are dilemmas we have probably all shared.

We want to be liked. We want to enjoy work and home life, and conflict does not help achieve this. So we try and avoid conflict, find a compromise and get on well. In my case I often choose to bury my head in a sand bucket, so to speak, and ignore potential issues for too long. The problem is when we become too friendly, there is a danger that this is seen as weakness or leniency and to get back to a place of authority takes a huge amount of effort and probably more than if we kept a stronger line on a constant basis.

I had this problem at work at this exact moment in time. I had three people in my team, all of whom were a similar age to me but motivated by different things. In order to get the best out of them, I tried to utilise their strengths and passions and I forgave and ignored certain behaviours that were inappropriate. There was one girl in particular who, after two and half years, I was really struggling with. Our relationship was strong but at times we were more like brother and sister than boss and employee. I had created this scenario and was really struggling to fix it.

I had to take a step back. I looked at parenting advice on how to discipline a child and I spoke to a number of colleagues about my problems at work. The similarities on how I was being advised to deal with both situations were quite surprising. It was comforting to realise that virtually all parents (and most line managers) have struggled with these issues. I realised that learning how to effectively discipline a child, is a skill that all parents have to learn. What I found interesting was the clear distinction between discipline and punishment with the former focusing on teaching. Discipline involves helping your child understand right from wrong, respect, acceptable behaviours and unacceptable behaviours. The aim is to help to develop a child to feel confident, self-disciplined and able to cope with frustration. Once I understood this and had reflected on how I dealt with these situations at home, I started to mirror my behaviour in the workplace and it proved effective.

Children will behave differently when they are not with their parents. According to her nursery, Jolie eats cream cheese sandwiches. According to my parents, when Jolie stays she is "a little angel". I wrote this part of the book in McDonalds on a Sunday afternoon and around me were three sets of grandparents with their grandchildren. Whilst some were struggling to get the kids to sit still and eat nicely, they were all having far more success than their parents would probably have in the same situation.

When I looked at myself to understand how I behaved when Jolie was naughty, I realised that when I gave in repeatedly if Jolie argued or had a tantrum then she was more likely to repeat the behaviour again and again. Being firm, fair and consistent helped her learn that in certain scenarios there was no point fighting as she was going to have to do it anyway (like bath time).

Elisa and I had to try and be more consistent with how we dealt with Jolie. This was a real challenge when my view was that I was at work and Jolie hadn't done anything to annoy or upset me, so why should I come home and discipline her? However, we soon realised that if we were not consistent then she would continue to misbehave for Elisa because daddy wouldn't mind and more importantly it was affecting the relationship that Elisa and Jolie shared. What happened as a result was that I was briefed by Elisa on my way home on whether Jolie had been good or bad and what Elisa had said, so I could be consistent when I arrived. Soon the gaps in our armour disappeared and Jolie found it much more difficult to play us against each other. When I looked at myself at work in a similar way I realised that I behaved differently with the different members of my team. Whilst, like children, every employee is different, and some adaptation is required, a consistent strength and style of discipline is vital to ensure everyone within the team feels like they are being treated fairly.

I think we forget sometimes that adults are a lot like children and are actually quite simple creatures. As a result, one of the easiest ways to get them to behave is to tell them up front what rewards or punishments will result from their good or bad behaviour respectively. With Jolie we remove TV, snacks, treats, going to the park etc. if she is naughty or we offer them in return for her behaving well (as she should anyway!) At work, the same type of behaviour seems to works well. Allowing the people who work for me to go on nights out, trips abroad linked to work, flexible hours and so on, keeps them motivated. The reverse also works. I once uninvited a member of my team from an awards dinner because they were not performing at the level I expected. Whilst this did not go down well at the time, the message was clear and the work almost immediately improved.

It is important to realise that there is a difference between rewards and bribes. A reward is something that you receive once you have done something whereas a bribe is given beforehand to motivate someone to do something you want. Bribes often involve money and are best to be avoided. However, rewards don't have to involve money. It is amazing how we can all be motivated by differing things. For some of us it's about recognition, for others financial reward. I once witnessed a colleague ask her boss if she could work half an hour for lunch and then leave half an hour early as she had an appointment. His response was "No". The result was that she became de-motivated, did nothing all day, except moan, and then left in a bad mood. I had a similar request shortly afterwards from one of my team. I decided the better response was to say of course he could leave early but not to worry about taking a shorter lunch break as he always worked more than his designated hours anyway. This led to a much more motivated and engaged member of staff.

Another example involved a crisis at work over Easter bank holiday. I was at the park with my children when I received a text from my boss about a serious incident. I had to immediately get up to speed and connect the right people in the business to the PR agency. When I got back to work my boss thanked me for being on call (even though it's part of my job) and gave me a bottle of wine as a thank you. This felt unnecessary but was hugely rewarding and motivating.

One of the most difficult things to do when Jolie or Fraser is naughty is to stay calm. At first it's easy to remain calm and placid but after asking or telling them to do something for the 25th time, it is really hard not to get cross and start shouting. The problem is that by me losing my temper, it implies that if they can't get me to do what they wants then it is ok for them to lose their temper and start shouting. If I find that

I am losing control then I take deep breaths, count to ten and if the worst comes to the worst, I get my wife to take over! At work, I sometimes find myself getting very annoyed with my team, colleagues or agencies who work with us and I have to try and stay calm. If I find myself writing a stroppy email, I generally don't send it immediately and re-read it before I do. If I find myself getting annoyed with my team, I try and have a chat with some trusted colleagues to make sure my perspective is fair, before I talk to them, calmly. Of course, there have been many occasions where I have hit send on an unfair email or unjustly reprimanded a member of staff and almost immediately regretted it.

Giving Jolie and Fraser feedback takes a lot more thought than I expected. I thought it would be as simple as telling them off when they did something naughty and praising them whenever they were good. However, my wife and I realised quite early on that we have to find the balance between being too critical and too positive. When we are critical of Jolie, we make sure that we are being critical of the behaviour and not of her. When praising Jolie, we try and make sure it is for things that are new and worth praising as opposed to everyday activities. We believe this makes the comments more effective. We also try and focus on positive reinforcement as opposed to continually highlighting the negatives. An example of this is when I get home from work and Elisa, in front of Jolie, tells me how good Jolie was when they were out.

Over the years I have learnt a number of things which have helped me give both positive and negative (or improvement) feedback designed to reinforce or change behaviour. When it comes to giving positive feedback, try to wait a little before giving it (e.g. a day) so that it feels considered and thought out as opposed to forced. Try to have any praise endorsed by a third party, give it consistently but avoid giving it if you are expecting something in return. It is always important to try and give as much positive feedback as negative, especially as our natural instinct is to focus on where people can improve. When giving the feedback itself, it is important to provide context, explain exactly what went well and what the impact was. Focus on what skills the staff member exhibited (especially ones you want to see more of) and end with congratulations and room for them to respond, if they so wish.

Giving negative or improvement feedback can be trickier, mainly because it makes most of us feel a little uncomfortable. We try to convince ourselves that we don't need to give this type of feedback and we put it off hoping the situation will resolve itself. This probably makes the problem even worse and giving feedback even more difficult. We should try to feedback as soon as possible after an incident but in an appropriate place, at an appropriate time. We have to try and be relaxed, use welcoming body language and a gentle tone whilst making sure we are feeding back trying to help, as opposed to because we are angry about something. In a similar way to providing positive feedback, it is important to provide context and explain the impact and why this matters. Explain specifically and non-judgementally what went wrong but try to reinforce their self confidence by pointing out situations where they had performed or behaved better yielding a better result. Discuss the issues and try and work through the potential options for a solution and improvement.

Something that children do that I think adults should do a lot more is actually ask for feedback. A number of times a day Jolie would ask me random questions from "Are you happy with me?" to "Is this right?" to "What do you think of my drawing?" to "What do you think of my new dress?" They are continually looking to learn and develop and if something isn't right, they want to know so they can fix it. Kids aren't afraid to ask for feedback but that attitude and openness gets repressed once we hit adulthood and we have to re-learn it. At work, asking for feedback can feel uncomfortable and can make your boss feel very put on the spot if you don't give them notice. However, it is a vital part of development, so make sure that your boss knows that you want feedback, ask open questions and find an appropriate place and time, possibly a specifically scheduled meeting.

We make the assumption that once feedback has been given, whether positive or negative, that it will be accepted and acted upon. Of course, this is often not the case. Sometimes, Jolie denies the feedback or claims that "It's not fair", sometimes she tries to explain her way out of it (e.g. "I drew on your wall because…") and sometimes she apologises and agrees, but I know she doesn't mean it and is only really saying it to get the topic over and done with. For example, Jolie has an amazing ability to say "I'm sorry", hugely convincingly and whilst at first we were fooled, over time we learnt when she meant it and when she didn't. To check we would ask if she understood why the subject was important and why it mattered. At work, my team all demonstrate a similar mix of responses from "No-one else thinks that" to "It wasn't my fault because" to "OK, fine". They even sometimes try and find hidden meaning in the feedback and try and draw me into a conversation about how I always wanted them to fail or I wanted them to leave.

I have found that the best solution in this scenario is to focus on the facts and not get sucked into an irrational emotional debate. It also helps to use third-party sources of information to demonstrate it is not a personal opinion. As an example, I had to feedback to one of my team about the fact that she was arriving at work too late. I have always been fairly comfortable with her arriving 30 minutes late as she always got her work done to a high standard and on time, she never left on time, we always got more than our fair share of hours and she was motivated and committed. However, when she started arriving 45 minutes to an hour late, it was setting a bad example to the rest of the department and I actually received feedback from senior management and so I had to take action. Whilst she accepted that she was late, she rationalised the feedback by pointing out that she got more done than anyone else and finished with a sham acceptance, "Whatever, I'll come in at 9am and leave at 5pm from now on". I then had to work through why the feedback was important and that it wasn't just my view. The outcome was that whilst she seldom arrived at or before 9am, she was very rarely more than 30 minutes late.

One of the major differences between work and home is that we can't fire our children (although sometimes we would probably like to!) Whilst, employees do not want to be considered their manager's children to be disciplined, similar tactics can work. As parents we will have a process for disciplining our children and we will often suspend or ban activities that they enjoy. Similarly, in any company, an official disciplinary procedure will exist. It is there to provide the company or your boss with a way of telling you when something is wrong. It allows them to explain the problem, what improvement or change in behaviour is needed and it should also give you an opportunity to explain your side of the story. Whilst sometimes the final result is dismissal, normally there is a process that a company has to go through before they get to this point. It starts with informally raising the issue, and then moves into a more formal process which can lead to a suspension or even dismissal, in the most serious of cases. With children, the process is not actually that different. Normally as a parent I begin by casually talking to Jolie about something she has done wrong. I explain the problem and why her behaviour isn't acceptable. If this doesn't solve the problem, I will move into a more formal process, normally involving the naughty step. If this doesn't help, then the activity will be suspended and if this still doesn't solve the problem then the activity is dismissed and banned.

Closing thoughts

I read a quote that said "While we try to teach our children all about life, our children teach us what life is all about". My children were the inspiration for this book and through parenting and watching them develop and grow I have learned so much.

This book has covered a variety of topics and has hopefully taken you as a reader on a journey of discovery. I started by comparing how we prepare for a new starter at work to how we prepare for a new baby entering our homes and lives. I looked at how we naturally manage our time better when our children demand it but how we struggle to do the same thing at work. I pointed out how we often don't encourage ourselves and others at work to learn new things but we are always trying to help our children learn and develop. I observed the benefits that could be derived from us harnessing a child's natural instinct to ask why and I talked about ways of improving, capturing and holding people's attention.

I used examples to show how children are brilliant negotiators and influencers and how the techniques they naturally exhibit are the same ones we try to re-learn as adults. I suggested that we drive fear into the hearts of our children and ourselves and then struggle to deal with it. I wondered about whether we could really care and listen to our teams and staff in the same way that we do to our children and loved ones and the difference this could make. And I finished by puzzling over how difficult it is to take and retain control.

My kids continue to push me out of my comfort zone and fuel my development as a father. I will be as likely to change when

Jolie and Fraser are teenagers as I did when they were toddlers'. Because I want to build strong sustainable relationships with my children, I will have to continually adapt my behaviour at home.

It has become obvious that the events that shape me as a person are as likely to come from home as they are from work and it will be experience rather than formal tuition that teaches me. I am sure that much of what I learn being a parent can continue to be transferred from playroom to boardroom.

As American television host Brian Tracy once said "If you raise your children to feel that they can accomplish any goal or task they decide upon, you will have succeeded as a parent and you will have given your children the greatest of all blessings". Consider this for your teams when you go into work next Monday morning.

About the author

Adam Margolin is the Head of Marketing and Management Information for SPAR in the UK. He previously worked in marketing for United Biscuits, General Mills and Unilever. He graduated from Leeds University with an International 1st Class Honours degree in Mathematics and Management Studies in 2003.

Adam is married with two children Jolie (four years old) and Fraser (one year old). Thinking about his comparative behaviour at home and at work led him to write this book.